Cooking Basics

RECIPES & TECHNIQUES

GENERAL EDITOR
CHUCK WILLIAMS

RECIPES
JACQUELINE MALLORCA

PHOTOGRAPHY
CHRIS SHORTEN

TIME
LIFE
BOOKS

Time-Life Books is a division of Time Life Inc.
Time-Life is a trademark of Time Warner Inc. U.S.A.

TIME-LIFE CUSTOM PUBLISHING

Vice President and Publisher: Terry Newell
Director of Sales: Neil Levin
Director of New Product Development: Regina Hall
Managing Editor: Donia Steele

WILLIAMS-SONOMA
Founder/Vice-Chairman: Chuck Williams

WELDON OWEN INC.
President: John Owen
Vice President and Publisher: Wendely Harvey
Vice President and CFO: Richard VanOosterhout
Associate Publisher: Laurie Wertz
Managing Editor: Lisa Chaney Atwood
Consulting Editor: Norman Kolpas
Copy Editor: Sharon Silva
Design: Angela Williams
Production Director: Stephanie Sherman
Production Coordinator: Tarji Mickelson
Production Editor: Janique Gascoigne
Editorial Assistant: Sarah Lemas
Co-Editions Director: Derek Barton
Food Photographer: Chris Shorten
Primary Food Stylist: Sue White
Technique Food Stylist: Andrea Lucich
Prop Stylist: Laura Ferguson
Assistant Prop Stylist: Danielle DiSalvo
Glossary Illustrations: Alice Harth

The Williams-Sonoma Kitchen Library
conceived and produced by Weldon Owen Inc.
814 Montgomery St., San Francisco, CA 94133

In collaboration with Williams-Sonoma
3250 Van Ness Ave., San Francisco, CA 94109

Production by Mandarin Offset, Hong Kong
Printed in China

A Note on Weights and Measures:
All recipes include customary U.S. and metric measurements. Metric conversions are based on a standard developed for these books and have been rounded off. Actual weights may vary.

A Weldon Owen Production

Copyright © 1996 Weldon Owen Inc.
All rights reserved, including the right of reproduction in whole or in part in any form.

Library of Congress
Cataloging-in-Publication Data:

Mallorca, Jacqueline.
    Cooking basics / general editor, Chuck Williams :
recipes, Jacqueline Mallorca ; photography, Chris Shorten.
        p.   cm. — (Williams-Sonoma kitchen library)
    Includes index.
    ISBN 0-7835-0318-0
    1. Cookery.   I. Williams, Chuck.   II. Title.   III. Series.
TX714.M3375   1996
641'.5—dc20   95-47663
                                                    CIP

Contents

INTRODUCTION

In every volume of the Williams-Sonoma Kitchen Library, it has been my intention to present good recipes in as simple and understandable a way as possible for experienced cooks and beginners alike. Indeed, in our busy modern times, a large generation has come of age without the benefit of learning to cook at the knee of their grandmothers or mothers. Culinary knowledge is no longer passed down as it was to generations in the past.

That's where this volume comes in. Each of its 48 recipes for good, basic, delicious dishes includes a short cooking lesson that teaches you—complete with step-by-step photographs—a useful cooking technique. As you cook your way through the book, you build a body of knowledge that can be tailored to whatever you like to prepare.

The recipes themselves are grouped into chapters by course and by featured ingredients, enabling you to compose a variety of simple menus. Think of it, if you like, as the equivalent of spending time in the kitchen with a trusted teacher who provides useful tips on preparing the family's meals.

I wanted this book to present the simple facts of cooking in a way that anyone could understand and use, regardless of his or her level of experience. In that goal, I think it succeeds. But only you can be the final judge, and I invite you to share your thoughts and reactions with me.

Chuck Williams

EQUIPMENT

From preparation to cooking, presentation to cleanup, essential kitchen tools get the job done

No matter what the level of your cooking expertise, having the right equipment at hand will make any recipe easier to prepare. That doesn't mean, however, that you need to stock your kitchen with an arsenal of cookware and tools. What is shown here demonstrates that it's more a matter of owning a few versatile basics.

1. Colander
For draining fresh produce after washing and vegetables, pasta and other ingredients after cooking.

2. Pastry Blender
For cutting butter or shortening into flour when making pastry dough or some cakes by hand.

3. Baking Sheets
Provides flat surfaces for baking breads, cookies and pastries. Select heavy aluminum or tinned steel. Dark, heavy-duty metal sheets conduct heat well for faster, more even browning.

4. Assorted Kitchen Tools
Crockery jar holds slotted spoon for removing and draining pieces of food from liquids; rubber spatula for folding ingredients together; wire whisk for beating egg whites, whipping cream and blending dressings and sauces; large metal spoon for stirring and basting; and wooden spatula and spoon for efficient mixing by hand and for stirring foods without harming the surfaces of cookware.

5. Vegetable Peeler
Slotted swiveling blade thinly strips away skins from vegetables and fruits.

6. Pepper Mill
Select a sturdy model with hardened-steel grinder.

7. Dutch Oven
For use on the stove top or in the oven, large-capacity enameled cast-iron cooking vessel—available in various sizes and shapes—with tight-fitting ovenproof lid.

8. Electric Stand Mixer
Heavy-duty countertop mixer with stainless-steel bowl. Attachments include a paddle for creaming butter and sugar; a whisk for beating batters, egg whites and cream; and a hook for kneading yeast doughs.

9. Potato Masher
For simple, quick mashing of potatoes and other cooked vegetables.

10. Saucepan
For all-purpose cooking.

11. Shallow Baking Dishes
Choose heavy, heatproof glass, porcelain or glazed earthenware.

12. Strainer
For all-purpose draining and straining. Fine wire mesh removes tiny particles of food from liquids.

13. Dry Measuring Cups
In graduated sizes, for accurate measuring of dry ingredients. Straight rims allow dry ingredients to be leveled accurately.

14. Metal Tongs
Spring-hinged, long tongs, for turning cuts of meat or poultry while cooking or browning.

15. Steamer Basket
Collapsible metal basket conforms to fit pans of various sizes, to hold food above the level of simmering liquid during steaming.

16. Measuring Spoons
In graduated sizes, for measuring small quantities of ingredients.

17. Tart Pan
Removable bottom of standard 9-inch (23-cm) pan allows tart to be easily unmolded. Fluted sides give pastry crust a sturdy and attractive edge.

18. Bulb Baster
Efficiently, safely suctions up pan juices for basting.

19. Liquid Measuring Cup
For accurate measuring of liquid ingredients. Choose heavy-duty heat-resistant glass, marked on one side in cups and ounces, on the other in milliliters. Lip and handle permit easy pouring.

20. Zester
Small, sharp holes at end of stainless-steel blade cut citrus zest into fine shreds.

21. Round Cake Pan
Usually comes in 8- and 9-inch (20- and 23-cm) sizes. Choose good-quality, seamless, heavy metal pans. Also available with removable bottom.

22. Box Grater
Four-sided, sturdy stainless-steel model for grating, shredding and slicing.

23. Food Processor
For chopping, slicing, puréeing or mixing ingredients quickly or in large quantities.

24. Stockpot
Deep, large-capacity pot with close-fitting lid, for making stock or for boiling or steaming large quantities of ingredients. Select a good-quality heavy pot that absorbs and transfers heat well.

25. Mixing Bowls
For easier mixing, choose deep bowls in a range of sizes. Lips and handles facilitate pouring.

26. Kitchen Scissors
For convenient, all-purpose cutting and trimming of ingredients.

27. Rolling Pin with Handles
The most commonly used rolling pin. Choose one with ball-bearing handles for smooth rolling, and a hardwood surface at least 12 inches (30 cm) long.

28. Broiler Pan
Cast-iron broiler pan with ridged surface elevates foods above any fats released during cooking.

29. Frying Pan
Choose good-quality, heavy cast iron, aluminum, stainless steel or enamel for rapid browning or frying.

30. Sauté Pan
Select a well-made heavy metal pan large enough to hold ingredients without crowding. Straight sides, usually about 2½ inches (6 cm) high, help contain splattering.

31. Loaf Pan
For baking loaves of quick or yeast-leavened bread, simple cakes and meat loaves. Metal pans conduct heat well.

32. Instant-Read Thermometer
Provides a quick and accurate measure of internal temperature when inserted into the thickest part of the item being cooked.

33. Mushroom Brush
Small, soft-bristled brush gently wipes dirt from the surface of fresh mushrooms.

34. Skimmer
Shallow fine-mesh strainer allows for removal of froth and scum from surface of stock and other simmering liquids; for lifting and draining solids from liquids or fried foods from hot oil.

35. Kitchen Towel
Good-quality cotton towel for general kitchen cleanup.

36. Pot Holder and Oven Mitt
Heavy-duty cotton, with one side treated for fire resistance, provides protection from hot cookware.

37. Ladle
For serving soups and stews, or for easy transferring of liquid or semiliquid mixtures.

THE BASICS OF COOKING

The following four pages present some of the most basic techniques of cooking, with step-by-step instructions on how to measure and clean ingredients, prepare seasonings, work with knives, carve roasted poultry and meat, and prepare a classic pan gravy.

Anyone learning to cook would do well to practice and master these fundamentals before moving on to the techniques presented with each recipe. Simple as these basics might seem, they will nonetheless make virtually any recipe you might prepare easier to do—and they will vastly improve the likelihood that you'll be happy with the results.

Even experienced cooks should review these steps from time to time. Like practice scales for a trained musician, they can contribute significantly to both the ease and artistry with which you perform.

MEASURING LIQUID & DRY INGREDIENTS

Accurate measuring of ingredients helps ensure that you achieve the desired results from any recipe. Baking, especially, relies on precise proportions of liquid to dry ingredients, and measuring can make the difference between success and failure.

Measuring liquids.
Measure liquid in a heavy-duty, heat-resistant glass measuring cup marked on one side with ounces, the other side with milliliters. Be sure to place the cup on a level surface and to read the measure at eye level for the most accuracy.

Measuring dry ingredients.
Spoon or, if directed, sift the dry ingredient—here, flour—into a straight-edged measuring cup. Draw the straight edge of a kitchen knife or spatula across the rim to level the ingredient for an accurate measurement.

CLEANING FRESH PRODUCE

Always take care to clean fruits and vegetables well before use to remove any dirt or residue from pesticides or preservatives. Rinsing under cold water is sufficient for most produce, although some—like those below—require more thorough cleansing.

Rinsing leeks.
Trim off the root end and tough green leaves from the leek. Cut it in half lengthwise. Hold under a stream of cold running water and separate the layers with your fingers to rinse out any grit trapped inside.

Rinsing fresh spinach.
Place fresh spinach leaves in a bowl, basin or sink filled with cold water. Swish well with your hands to rinse off the dirt. Lift out the leaves and drain away the water. Repeat until no dirt remains in the water when the leaves are removed.

ADDING FLAVOR

The following techniques will help you extract the most flavor from four common seasonings that add great character to recipes.

Zesting citrus fruit.
For thin strips of citrus zest, draw the sharp-edged holes of a zester—shown here— across the surface of a whole citrus fruit. Alternatively, use the small indented slots on a fine-holed shredder.

Grating whole nutmeg.
Grate nutmeg just before use, rubbing the whole nutmeg against the rasps of a small grater. The special nutmeg grater shown here includes a compartment in which the whole spice can be stored.

Peeling garlic cloves.
To remove the papery skin from a garlic clove, place the clove on a work surface and cover with the side of a large knife. Press down on the blade to crush the clove slightly. The skin will slip off.

Crushing dried herbs.
Crushing releases the flavor of dried herbs before they are added to a recipe. Simply rub them between your fingertips, as shown; or hold them in one palm and crush with the thumb of the other hand.

BASIC KNIFE TECHNIQUES

Equip your kitchen with a good set of professional-quality knives, with sharp, stainless-steel blades securely attached to sturdy handles that feel comfortable in your hand. Kept well sharpened and handled correctly, as shown here, they will work efficiently and will be far less likely to cause injury.

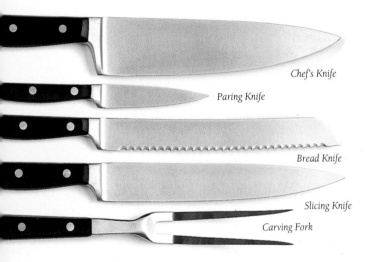

Chef's Knife

Paring Knife

Bread Knife

Slicing Knife

Carving Fork

SLICING

Steady the food being sliced with your free hand, tucking your fingertips inward towards your palm away from the knife blade, and keeping the side of the blade against your knuckles.

Cutting into slices.
Place the food—here, an onion, cut in half so it sits securely—on the work surface. Carefully steadying the onion with one hand, use the knife to cut uniform slices of the desired thickness, guiding the blade with the knuckles of your safely underturned fingers.

DICING

When dicing foods other than the onion shown here, cut uniform slices; stack them, cut again to make strips, and then cut across the strips to make cubes.

Dicing an onion.
Using an 8–10-inch (20–25-cm) chef's knife, cut the onion in half through the stem end and place cut-side down on the work surface. Make parallel vertical slices from the stem end to within about ½ inch (12 mm) of the root end. Cut across the slices (left) to make uniform cubes.

CHOPPING

Essential to chopping is a good cutting surface and a chef's knife about 8–10 inches (20–25 cm) in length, the shape of which permits the rhythmic rocking motion shown here.

Chopping coarsely to finely.
Cut the item to be chopped into coarse pieces. Grasp the handle of a chef's knife and, with your other hand, steady the top of the blade near its tip. Raise and lower the handle in a chopping motion, slowly swinging the blade back and forth across the food; continue until the desired texture is achieved.

MINCING

Similar to chopping, although on a smaller scale, mincing is done most efficiently with a small chef's knife.

Cutting fine pieces.
Using a 6–8-inch (15–20-cm) chef's knife, cut the food—here, garlic cloves—into thin slices. Then cut crosswise into thin strips and crosswise again into small cubes. Apply the same motion used for chopping (above) to mince the food to the desired fineness.

CARVING POULTRY

You don't need a degree in anatomy to carve poultry. Do it once or twice, following these instructions, and you'll have it mastered. After you've trussed the bird and roasted it properly (pages 51–52), let it rest for a few minutes so the juices can settle before carving.

1. Removing the legs.
Cut off the trussing strings. Pull the whole leg away from the body and, using a knife, cut through the skin between the thigh and body to locate the joint. Cut through the joint to free the leg. Repeat with the other leg. Remove the wings in the same way, if desired, cutting through the shoulder joint where it meets the breast.

2. Slicing the breast meat.
Steadying the bird with a carving fork, use a carving knife to cut away the breast meat in uniform slices at about a 45-degree angle. Large breasts, such as those from a large chicken or turkey, are commonly sliced as shown; smaller breasts are often removed whole by cutting down between the meat and breastbone and then along the ribcage.

SLICING MEAT

A good, sharp, thin-bladed, slightly flexible slicing knife enables you to cut thin, uniform slices of meat without loss of juices or texture.

Slicing across the grain.
Cutting meat across the grain highlights its texture and makes individual servings easier for the diner to cut on the plate. For the best slicing technique, steady the meat with a carving fork and use a slicing knife to cut the meat across the grain into slices of the desired thickness.

MAKING GRAVY

The secret of lump-free gravy lies in preparing a flour-and-fat roux, vigorously stirring in liquid and straining before serving.

1. Pouring off the fat.
While the roast rests before carving, pick up the roasting pan with pot holders and carefully pour off all but 3–5 tablespoons of the fat.

2. Adding the flour.
Place the roasting pan over medium heat. Sprinkle in 1–3 tablespoons all-purpose (plain) flour, stirring rapidly to incorporate it with the fat and pan juices and to break up any lumps. Cook briefly, stirring, until lightly browned.

3. Adding the stock.
Raise the heat to high and, stirring vigorously, pour in hot stock and bring to a boil. Reduce the heat to medium and simmer, stirring often, for 5 minutes. Stir in more stock if necessary to achieve a saucelike consistency.

4. Straining the gravy.
Season the gravy to taste with salt and pepper. Pour through a fine-mesh sieve into a warmed gravy boat, stir in a tablespoon of minced fresh herb (if using) and serve hot.

SEEDING AND DERIBBING LARGE CHILIES
Prepare large chilies for stuffing by cutting around the stem and then pulling it and the attached seed cluster free. Tap out any loose seeds, then remove the white ribs.

SEEDING AND DERIBBING SMALL CHILIES
Cut the chili in half lengthwise. Use the tip of a paring knife to cut out the seed cluster and thin, white ribs.

Stuffed Poblano Chilies

Wear rubber gloves and be careful not to touch your eyes when handling chilies to protect against the volatile oils present in the seeds and ribs.

4 fresh poblano chili peppers
¼ lb (125 g) blue cheese, crumbled
¼ lb (125 g) Monterey Jack cheese, shredded
¼ lb (125 g) sharp Cheddar cheese, shredded
2 tablespoons olive oil

FOR THE JALAPEÑO SALSA:
2 ripe tomatoes

salt
1 fresh jalapeño chili pepper
3 green (spring) onions, chopped
3 tablespoons chopped fresh cilantro (fresh coriander)
½ teaspoon ground cumin
juice of 1 lemon
¼ cup (2 fl oz/60 ml) olive oil
freshly ground pepper

*P*reheat an oven to 400°F (200°C). Remove the stems and seeds from the poblanos (see top photo). Cut off the cluster of seeds, but reserve the caps with stems intact. Fill a saucepan three-fourths full with water and bring to a boil. Boil the peppers for 2 minutes. Using a slotted spoon, transfer to cold water to cool; drain and blot dry.

In a bowl, combine the cheeses. Stuff the peppers; replace the caps. Pour the oil into a baking dish and roll the peppers in it, then lay them on their sides. Cover with aluminum foil and bake until tender when pierced with a knife, about 30 minutes.

Meanwhile, make the salsa: Peel and seed the tomatoes (see page 22). Sprinkle the tomato halves with salt. Place, cut sides down, in a colander to drain, about 20 minutes, then dice.

Meanwhile, remove the seeds and ribs from the jalapeño chili (see bottom photo). Chop finely and place in a bowl. Add the green onions, cilantro, cumin, lemon juice, oil and tomatoes. Toss to mix; season to taste with salt and pepper.

Transfer the baked chili peppers to warmed plates and top with the salsa. Serve immediately.

Serves 4

PREPARING & PEELING
BELL PEPPERS

STEMMING, SEEDING AND DERIBBING
Grab the seed cluster from the center of the
cut peppers and pull it and the stem free,
then remove the white ribs.

PEELING ROASTED PEPPERS
Using your fingers or a small, sharp knife,
peel away the skins from the roasted
peppers.

Marinated Bell Peppers

*Most varieties of bell peppers turn red or yellow when mature, and
develop a sweet, mellow flavor. Their tough (and indigestible) skin
can be removed by exposing it to high heat and then peeling it off.*

2 red bell peppers (capsicums)	3 tablespoons olive oil
2 yellow bell peppers (capsicums)	1 large clove garlic, minced
6 anchovy fillets in olive oil, drained and chopped	2 heads Belgian endive (chicory/witloof), leaves separated (optional)
freshly ground black pepper	fresh basil leaves (optional)
salt	buttered, toasted baguette slices (optional)
1 tablespoon drained capers	

Preheat a broiler (griller). Line a broiler pan with parchment
paper or aluminum foil, if desired, to keep the pan free of any
burned-on juices. Cut the peppers lengthwise into quarters, then
remove the stems, seeds and ribs (see top photo). Arrange the
quarters, cut sides down, on the prepared broiler pan. Broil (grill)
about 4 inches (10 cm) below the heat source until the skins
blacken and blister, 5–6 minutes. Remove from the broiler, cover
with aluminum foil and let stand for 10 minutes, then peel away
the skins (see bottom photo).

Preheat an oven to 400°F (200°C). Cut each quarter lengthwise
into 4 strips. Scatter half over the bottom of a large, shallow baking
dish. Sprinkle evenly with the anchovies, black pepper to taste, a
little salt, capers, half of the olive oil and the garlic. Top with the
remaining peppers and drizzle with the remaining oil. Bake until
the peppers have softened, about 15 minutes. Let cool.

To serve, spoon the peppers into the larger endive leaves, reserv-
ing the smaller leaves for another use; or transfer the peppers to a
plate, garnish with basil leaves and serve with baguette slices.

Makes about 16; serves 4

TRIMMING BABY ARTICHOKES

1. REMOVING THE OUTER LEAVES
Bend each tough leaf downward until it snaps off, removing 3 or 4 layers to reveal the tender inner core. Transfer to a bowl of water and lemon juice to prevent discoloring.

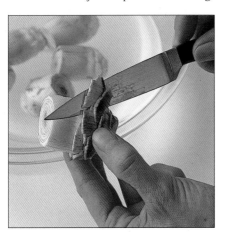

2. TRIMMING THE ARTICHOKE
After removing the leaves and cutting off the artichoke top, cut away the dark green, tough, fibrous outer layer covering the base.

Baby Artichokes in Prosciutto

Artichokes are the immature, thick-petalled flowers of an edible thistle; baby artichokes are the buds. As they have not yet developed a fuzzy choke, the small artichoke buds need only a light trimming of their outer leaves before they can be eaten whole.

1 lemon, cut into wedges
1 lb (500 g) baby artichokes
2 cups (16 fl oz/500 ml) chicken stock *(recipe on page 21)*
2 teaspoons white wine vinegar
pinch of salt
freshly ground pepper
3 tablespoons olive oil
2 green (spring) onions, white part only, finely chopped
¼ lb (125 g) very thinly sliced prosciutto

Squeeze the juice from the lemon wedges into a large bowl of water; discard the lemon.

Remove the tough outer leaves of each artichoke and place the prepared bud in the bowl of lemon water until all are done (Step 1). Using a sharp knife, cut off the top third of the artichoke, then cut off the stem flush with the base. Trim away the fibrous green layer around the base (Step 2). Cut any larger artichokes in half lengthwise. As you work, return trimmed artichokes to the lemon water.

In a saucepan over medium heat, bring the stock to a boil. Drain the artichokes, add them to the stock and return to a boil. Reduce the heat to low and simmer until tender when pierced with a knife, about 7 minutes.

Meanwhile, in a shallow bowl, combine the vinegar and salt and stir to dissolve. Add pepper to taste. Whisk in the olive oil until a thick emulsion forms. Stir in the green onions.

Drain the artichokes and add them to the bowl. Toss to coat well. When cool, wrap each artichoke in a short strip of prosciutto and secure with a toothpick. Arrange on a platter or individual plates and serve.

Serves 4

PURÉEING VEGETABLES

PURÉEING FOR A COARSE TEXTURE
Spoon the cooked vegetables into a food mill fitted with the coarse or medium disk set atop a mixing bowl. Turn the crank to purée the vegetables, adding a little broth if needed.

PURÉEING FOR A SMOOTH TEXTURE
Spoon the cooked vegetables into a food processor fitted with the metal blade, and process until evenly smooth.

Cream of Carrot Soup

If you prefer coarser textured soups, purée with a food mill fitted with the coarse or medium disk; or for smoother soups, use the steady blending of a food processor or blender. If a food mill is unavailable, use the pulsing action of a food processor or blender to purée ingredients to a coarse texture.

2 tablespoons unsalted butter
1 yellow onion, diced
1 clove garlic, finely chopped
6 carrots, 1¼ lb (625 g), peeled and diced
2 cups (16 fl oz/500 ml) chicken stock (*recipe on page 21*)

salt and ground white pepper
1¼ cups (10 fl oz/310 ml) low-fat milk
½ cup (¾ oz/20 g) chopped fresh cilantro (fresh coriander)

*I*n a saucepan over medium-low heat, melt the butter. Add the onion and garlic, cover and reduce the heat to very low. Cook, stirring occasionally, until tender but not browned, about 10 minutes. Add the carrots and chicken stock and season to taste with salt and a generous sprinkling of white pepper. Bring to a boil, then reduce the heat to low. Cover partially and simmer until the carrots are tender, about 20 minutes.

Working in batches and using a slotted spoon, transfer the carrot mixture to a food mill or a food processor. Purée the carrots to the desired consistency (see techniques at left). When all the carrots are puréed, stir them back into the broth remaining in the saucepan.

Place the saucepan over medium-low heat, add the milk and heat gently, stirring. Add the cilantro, stir well, then taste and adjust the seasonings. Ladle into warmed bowls and serve hot.

Serves 4

SKIMMING & DEGREASING

SKIMMING A SIMMERING LIQUID
As the liquid—here, chicken stock—begins to reach a simmer, use a wire skimmer to remove the froth that rises to its surface. Continue skimming until no more forms.

DEGREASING WITH A LARGE SPOON
Use a large spoon to skim off the fat that has risen to the top. Draw a paper towel over the top to absorb any remaining fat.

Homemade Chicken Stock

This recipe for chicken stock forms the basis for a variety of chicken soups. Suggestions for three favorites follow.

4 lb (2 kg) chicken wings and backs
2 whole chicken legs, with thighs attached
2½ qt (2.5 l) cold water
1 yellow onion, cut into chunks
3 celery stalks, cut into chunks
2 carrots, cut into chunks
1 leek, carefully rinsed
1 bay leaf
6 peppercorns
6 fresh parsley sprigs

Place all the chicken pieces in a large pot and add the water. Bring to a boil, skimming off any froth that forms on the surface (see top photo). Reduce the heat to low, cover partially and simmer gently for 1 hour, skimming the stock several more times.

If using the stock for soup, remove the chicken legs, skin them, remove the meat and dice; set aside. Return the skin and bones to the pot.

Add the onion, celery, carrots, leek, bay leaf, peppercorns and parsley to the pot. Cover partially and continue to simmer gently for 3 hours longer.

Pour the stock through a sieve placed over a bowl. Let cool, then remove the fat by spooning it from the surface (see bottom photo) or chilling the stock until the fat congeals and then lifting it off.

Use the stock in any recipe calling for chicken stock, or reheat the stock and add a selection of your favorite ingredients to make soup. For cream of chicken soup, add 2 cups (16 fl oz/500 ml) heated heavy (double) cream. For chicken noodle soup, add 1½ cups (9 oz/270 g) cooked egg noodles. For chicken rice soup, add 6 tablespoons white rice to the simmering stock and simmer until tender, about 20 minutes. Finish any of the soups with the addition of the reserved diced cooked chicken, salt and ground white pepper to taste, and a sprinkling of chopped fresh parsley.

Makes about 8 cups (64 fl oz/2 l) stock; serves 6–8

PEELING & SEEDING TOMATOES

1. SCORING THE SKIN
Using a small knife, cut out the core then cut a shallow X in the base of a tomato.

2. PEELING THE TOMATOES
Blanch in boiling water for 15–20 seconds. Lift out with a slotted spoon and transfer to ice water. Starting at the X, peel off the skin.

3. SEEDING THE TOMATOES
Squeeze a tomato half over a bowl or sink to force out the seeds. Use a fingertip or a small spoon to clean out any stray seeds.

Fresh Tomato Soup

Removing the skin and seeds from fresh tomatoes before adding them to soup ensures a smooth, concentrated texture.

2 lb (1 kg) ripe tomatoes
2 tablespoons unsalted butter
1 yellow onion, finely diced
½ cup (¾ oz/20 g) chopped celery leaves
1 bay leaf
2 cups (16 fl oz/500 ml) chicken stock (*recipe on page 21*)

salt and ground white pepper
2 tablespoons cornstarch (cornflour)
1 cup (8 fl oz/250 ml) low-fat milk
1 tablespoon chopped fresh oregano

Fill a saucepan three-fourths full with water and bring to a boil. Cut out the core from the stem end of each tomato, then cut a shallow X in the base (Step 1). Blanch the tomatoes for 15–20 seconds, then peel (Step 2) and seed (Step 3). Cut the tomatoes into large dice; there should be about 3 cups (18 oz/560 g).

In a heavy-bottomed saucepan over medium heat, melt the butter. Add the onion, celery leaves and bay leaf, cover, reduce the heat to very low and cook until softened but not browned, about 10 minutes. Add the tomatoes and chicken stock and season to taste with salt and white pepper. Bring to a boil, reduce the heat to low, cover partially and simmer, stirring occasionally, until the flavors have blended, about 30 minutes. Discard the bay leaf.

In a small bowl, stir the cornstarch into the milk until dissolved and then add to the hot soup. Simmer, stirring, for 5 minutes. The soup will thicken and lighten in color. Stir in the oregano, then taste and adjust the seasonings. Ladle into warmed bowls and serve hot.

Serves 4–6

SECTIONING CITRUS FRUIT

1. CUTTING OFF THE PEEL
Stand the orange upright. Following the contour of the fruit, slice off the peel, pith and membrane in thick strips.

2. CUTTING OUT THE SECTIONS
Holding the fruit over a bowl, cut along each side of the membrane between the sections, letting each freed section drop into the bowl.

Orange and Fennel Salad

Fennel is a pale green, bulbous vegetable with feathery tops and a delicious licoricelike flavor. Sweet orange slices, trimmed of their bitter skin and pith, offer a perfect foil to fennel's assertive taste.

4 navel oranges or large
   Valencia oranges
4 small fennel bulbs, about
   1½ lb (750 g) total
2 green (spring) onions, white
   part only, thinly sliced

2 cups (2 oz/60 g) loosely
   packed baby spinach leaves,
   carefully rinsed and dried
1 tablespoon red wine vinegar
⅛ teaspoon salt
freshly ground pepper
¼ cup (2 fl oz/60 ml) olive oil

Using a small, sharp knife, cut off a slice from the top and bottom of each orange, removing all the membrane to reveal the flesh. Then cut off the peel from each orange (Step 1). Holding the fruit over a bowl to catch the juices, cut away the orange sections, letting them drop into the bowl and rotating the orange as you work (Step 2). If using Valencia oranges, pick out and discard any seeds. Finally, squeeze any remaining juice from the empty membranes into the bowl before discarding the membranes.

Trim off any feathery tops from the fennel bulbs and discard. Cut away any discolored areas from the bulbs. Cut the bulbs and tender stalks crosswise into very thin slices and add to the orange sections along with the green onions. Divide the spinach leaves among 4 salad plates.

In a small bowl, combine the vinegar and salt and stir to dissolve the salt. Add pepper to taste and then slowly whisk in the olive oil to form an emulsion. Pour the vinaigrette over the orange mixture and toss gently. Spoon over the spinach leaves, dividing evenly, and serve.

Serves 4

MAKING VINAIGRETTE

1. DISSOLVING SALT IN VINEGAR
Add the salt to the vinegar. Using a small whisk or a fork, stir to dissolve the salt.

2. MAKING AN EMULSION
Add the oil to the vinegar in a slow, steady stream while beating vigorously with the whisk or fork until an emulsion forms.

Tossed Green Salad with Vinaigrette

The classic vinaigrette combines 1 part vinegar to 4 or more parts oil, depending upon the tartness of the vinegar. Herbs, mustard or anchovy can be added for extra flavor. Include any variety of fresh salad greens such as butter lettuce, frisée (mizuna), red leaf lettuce, arugula (rocket), oak leaf lettuce, and mixed baby lettuces.

4 cups (4 oz/125 g) loosely
  packed, assorted salad greens
  (see note)
1 tablespoon wine vinegar

⅛–¼ teaspoon salt
freshly ground pepper
¼ cup (2 fl oz/60 ml) olive oil,
  preferably extra-virgin

Rinse the salad greens thoroughly, drain and spin dry in a salad spinner or blot dry between 2 kitchen towels. Tear into bite-sized pieces, if necessary, and place in a bowl.

Pour the vinegar into a small bowl, add the salt to taste and stir to dissolve (Step 1). Add pepper to taste and then whisk in the olive oil (Step 2).

Pour the vinaigrette evenly over the salad greens and toss gently to coat evenly. Serve immediately.

Serves 4

Vinaigrette with Mustard: Beat in 1 teaspoon Dijon or other good-quality prepared mustard or ½ teaspoon dry mustard with the pepper.
Vinaigrette with Herbs: Stir in 1 teaspoon finely chopped fresh parsley, chives, chervil or tarragon with the pepper.
Vinaigrette with Anchovy: Omit the salt. Drain 2 anchovy fillets that have been packed in olive oil, then crush with a spoon to a paste. Stir in the anchovy paste with the pepper.

GRATING, SHREDDING & SHAVING CHEESE

GRATING AND SHREDDING HARD CHEESE
Use the small grating holes of a box grater (left) for grated cheese. Use the larger holes for shredded cheese (right).

SHAVING HARD CHEESE
Hold a block of cheese directly over dish. Firmly draw a vegetable peeler or cheese plane evenly across its surface.

Blacksmith Salad

This oddly named salad was created in Modena, the ancient Italian city that gave the world balsamic vinegar. It is traditionally topped with Parmesan, although any type of hard or semihard cheese can be used. The cheese can be either grated, shredded or shaved into paper-thin slices.

3 small heads butter (Boston) lettuce
3 oz (90 g) hard or semihard cheese such as Parmesan, Asiago or Gruyère
2 tablespoons good-quality balsamic vinegar

pinch of salt
3 tablespoons olive oil, preferably extra-virgin
1½ cups (3 oz/90 g) homemade croutons

Discard any tough or discolored outer leaves from the lettuce heads, then separate the leaves from the heads. Rinse thoroughly, drain and spin dry in a salad spinner or blot dry between kitchen towels. Tear the large leaves in half, and place all the lettuce in a salad bowl.

Sprinkle the vinegar and salt over the lettuce and toss well to mix. Drizzle with the olive oil, scatter the croutons over the top and toss again.

Shave, grate or shred the cheese to use as a garnish (see techniques at left). If using grated or shredded cheese, sprinkle it over the lettuce. If using shaved cheese, shave it directly over the salad.

Serve immediately.

Serves 6

PREPARING DRIED BEANS

SORTING THE BEANS
Spread the dried beans in a single layer on a work surface and sort through them to remove any damaged beans or stones.

SOAKING THE BEANS
To rehydrate the beans for more even cooking, place them in a bowl, add water to cover by 2–3 inches (5–7.5 cm) and let soak for about 3 hours.

Mixed Bean Pot with Pancetta

If dried chick-peas are hard to find, use 3 cups (21 oz/655 g) drained, canned chick-peas, mixing them into the cooked kidney and white beans.

1 cup (7 oz/220 g) dried red kidney beans
1 cup (7 oz/220 g) dried small white (navy) beans
1 cup (7 oz/220 g) dried chick-peas (garbanzo beans)
2 cups (16 fl oz/500 ml) chicken stock *(recipe on page 21)*
1 tablespoon olive oil
¼ lb (125 g) pancetta, chopped
2 yellow onions, sliced
3 cloves garlic, minced
1 teaspoon dried thyme

1 teaspoon dried sage
3-inch (7.5-cm) strip orange zest pierced with 4 whole cloves
1 can (14½ oz/455 g) chopped tomatoes, with their juices
1–2 teaspoons salt
freshly ground pepper
1 cup (4 oz/125 g) fresh bread crumbs tossed with 2 table-spoons melted unsalted butter
fresh sage sprig

Sort through the beans (see top photo), rinse and soak (see bottom photo). Drain the beans, place in a large saucepan and add the stock and hot water to cover by 1 inch (2.5 cm). Bring to a boil, reduce the heat to low, cover and simmer gently until tender, about 1 hour.

Preheat an oven to 350°F (180°C). In a large frying pan over medium heat, warm the oil. Add the pancetta and sauté until lightly cooked, about 5 minutes. Using a slotted spoon, transfer to a small bowl; reserve. Add the onions, garlic, thyme and sage to the same pan, cover and cook over medium-low heat until soft, 6–7 minutes. Stir in the beans and chick-peas and their liquid, the pancetta, orange zest with cloves and tomatoes with juices. Season to taste with salt and pepper and bring to a boil.

Transfer the bean mixture to a deep baking dish and top with the buttered bread crumbs. Bake until browned, about 30 minutes. Garnish with the sage sprig and serve hot.

Serves 6–8

COOKING RICE

COOKING WILD RICE
Cook wild rice slowly until the grains have split open and are tender but still chewy. Pour off any liquid that remains in the pan.

COOKING WHITE RICE
Cook white rice slowly until the grains are fluffy and dry when lifted with a fork and no liquid remains. Do not lift the lid during cooking to ensure that the rice steams to an even and dry consistency.

White and Wild Rice Pilaf

White rice is best cooked in a small amount of water to a dry, fluffy consistency. Wild rice, on the other hand, is boiled to a moist, chewy consistency, then drained of any excess liquid.

FOR WILD RICE:
3 cups (24 fl oz/750 ml) chicken stock *(recipe on page 21)*
¼ teaspoon salt, if using unsalted stock
1 cup (6 oz/185 g) wild rice, well rinsed

FOR WHITE RICE:
1 cup (7 oz/220 g) long-grain white, jasmine or basmati rice
2 cups (16 fl oz/500 ml) water
¾ teaspoon salt

6 tablespoons unsalted butter
1 cup (4 oz/125 g) toasted pecans, chopped

To cook the wild rice, pour the stock into a 1½-qt (1.5-l) saucepan with a tight-fitting lid. Bring to a boil over high heat and add the salt, if using. Add the rice slowly, so the liquid continues to boil. Stir once, cover, reduce the heat to low and simmer gently until the liquid evaporates and the grains have split open and are tender (see top photo), 45–50 minutes. Drain off any excess liquid, if necessary.

About 25 minutes before the wild rice is done, cook the white rice. (If using basmati rice, rinse well and drain.) Pour the water into another 1½-qt (1.5-l) saucepan with a tight-fitting lid. Bring to a boil over high heat and add the salt. Add the rice slowly, so the liquid continues to boil. Stir once, cover, reduce the heat to low and simmer gently until the liquid evaporates and the grains are separate and fluffy (see bottom photo), about 20 minutes.

In a large bowl, mix together the wild and white rice. Stir in the butter and the pecans and serve.

Makes about 5 cups (30 oz/940 g); serves 6–8

MAKING RISOTTO

SAUTÉING THE RICE
Sauté the rice over medium heat, stirring, until the edge of each kernel becomes slightly translucent.

ADDING THE LIQUID
A little at a time, add hot liquid to the rice and stir over medium-low heat until fully absorbed before adding more.

Risotto with Saffron

Always use Arborio rice when making risotto; the round grains cook to a creamy yet firm consistency that is unattainable with other types of rice. It is also important to add the stock a little at a time so that the grains swell slowly and evenly. Garnish with parsley, if you like.

2 cups (16 fl oz/500 ml) chicken stock *(recipe on page 21)*
2–2½ cups (16–20 fl oz/ 500–625 ml) water
6 tablespoons (3 oz/90 g) unsalted butter
2 tablespoons olive oil
1 yellow onion, finely chopped

2 tablespoons finely chopped prosciutto or pancetta
1 cup (7 oz/220 g) Italian Arborio rice
large pinch of saffron threads
¾ cup (3 oz/90 g) freshly grated Parmesan cheese
salt and freshly ground pepper

*I*n a saucepan over medium heat, combine the chicken stock and 2 cups (16 fl oz/500 ml) of the water to make a light stock. Heat to a low simmer.

In a large, heavy saucepan over medium heat, melt 4 tablespoons (2 oz/60 g) of the butter with the olive oil. Add the onion and prosciutto or pancetta and sauté, stirring, until the onion is soft, about 5 minutes. Add the rice and stir until slightly translucent (see top photo), 1–2 minutes.

Start adding the hot stock, ½ cup (4 fl oz/125 ml) at a time, stirring continuously. Continue to cook over medium-low heat, stirring frequently and gradually adding more stock (see bottom photo).

After 20 minutes, dissolve the saffron threads in the remaining simmering stock and continue adding the stock to the rice until creamy and the grains are tender to the bite, 5–10 minutes longer; if needed, add the remaining ½ cup (4 fl oz/125 ml) water, first brought to a simmer. Stir in the cheese and the remaining 2 tablespoons butter. Season to taste with salt and pepper. Serve at once.

Serves 4 as a first course, 2–3 as a main course

COOKING POLENTA

ADDING POLENTA TO SIMMERING WATER
Stirring constantly, add the polenta to the
simmering water in a thin, steady stream
to prevent the grains from clumping.

COOKING THE POLENTA
Cook, stirring over the bottom and to the
pan sides with a wooden spatula, until the
polenta is thick, creamy and begins to pull
from the pan sides.

Polenta with Tomato Sauce

2 tablespoons olive oil
1 yellow onion, chopped
3 cloves garlic, minced
3 cups (18 oz/560 g) peeled,
  seeded (*see page 22*) and
  chopped tomatoes with
  their juices
3–4 tablespoons tomato paste
2 teaspoons sugar
1 tablespoon chopped fresh
  basil
½ teaspoon ground pepper
salt
6½ cups (52 fl oz/1.6 l) water
2 cups (10 oz/315 g) polenta
  or coarse yellow cornmeal
olive oil, if frying the polenta
2 oz (60 g) thinly sliced prosciutto, coarsely chopped
fresh basil sprigs, optional
freshly grated Parmesan cheese

*I*n a heavy-bottomed saucepan over medium heat, warm the olive
oil. Add the onion and garlic and sauté, stirring, until soft, 5–6
minutes. Stir in the tomatoes, tomato paste, sugar, basil, pepper,
and salt to taste. Bring to a boil, then reduce the heat to low and
simmer, uncovered, until thickened, 30–40 minutes.

Meanwhile, in a deep, heavy saucepan over high heat, bring the
water to a boil. Add 1 tablespoon salt. Reduce the heat to low so
the water simmers, and stir in the polenta (see top photo). Cook,
stirring, for about 20 minutes (see bottom photo).

If soft polenta is preferred, simply spoon a bed of the polenta into
warmed shallow bowls.

If polenta squares are preferred, spread the hot polenta in a greased,
rimmed baking sheet, forming a layer ½ inch (12 mm) thick. Let
cool until set, then cut into squares. In a large sauté pan over high
heat, pour in olive oil to a depth of ½ inch (12 mm). Working in
batches, fry the squares, turning once, until crispy but not
browned, 4–6 minutes.

Top the soft polenta or polenta squares with the tomato sauce
and the prosciutto. Garnish with basil, if using, and Parmesan.

Serves 4–6

DRAINING PASTA
Holding the pot with pot holders, pour the pasta and boiling water into a colander placed in the sink.

TOSSING PASTA AND SAUCE
Immediately after draining, while water still clings to it, add the pasta to the prepared sauce. Toss well.

Pasta Primavera

In Italian, primavera means "spring," so this fresh-tasting sauce should be made with the first tiny vegetables of the season. After draining the pasta, add it to the sauce while it is still slightly wet; the hot pasta will continue to absorb moisture, enabling it to become evenly coated with sauce.

3 tablespoons unsalted butter
½ cup (2½ oz/75 g) diagonally sliced asparagus tips
½ cup (2½ oz/75 g) baby green beans
½ cup (2½ oz/75 g) small peas
½ cup (2½ oz/75 g) sliced yellow summer squash
¾ cup (6 fl oz/180 ml) heavy (double) cream
salt
freshly ground pepper
4 qt (4 l) water
1 teaspoon olive oil
1 lb (500 g) dried fettuccine or spaghetti
freshly grated Italian Parmesan cheese

*I*n a large sauté pan over medium heat, melt the butter. Add the asparagus, beans, peas and squash and sauté, stirring, until tender-crisp, about 5 minutes. Add the cream and season to taste with salt and pepper. Boil briskly, stirring for 1–2 minutes to reduce slightly. Remove from the heat and cover to keep warm.

Meanwhile, in a large pot over high heat, bring the water to a rolling boil. Add 1 teaspoon salt and the olive oil to the boiling water to prevent the pasta from sticking together. Add the pasta, stirring gently. Boil, stirring occasionally, until *al dente* (tender but still firm to the bite), 6–10 minutes or according to package directions.

Drain the pasta in a colander (see top photo) and, acting quickly, immediately add it to the cooked sauce (see bottom photo). Toss well and promptly divide among warmed plates. Top with Parmesan cheese.

Serves 4

SEARING FISH FILLETS

COOKING IN A HOT PAN
Cook fish until seared to an opaque off-white on the first side; turn with metal tongs (to avoid piercing and losing juices) to sear the second side.

TESTING FISH FOR DONENESS
Use a fork or knife to split open along the grain. It should be red for rare.

Seared Tuna with Sweet Balsamic Onions

Searing is accomplished by quickly cooking meat over medium-high heat to seal the surface and thus retain the juices without really browning the meat. Because it is popularly cooked rare, the firm, red flesh of fresh ahi tuna is particularly well suited to the searing technique.

2 tablespoons olive oil
2 cups (7 oz/220 g) thinly sliced yellow onion
2 teaspoons sugar
salt and freshly ground pepper
⅓ cup (3 fl oz/80 ml) red wine vinegar

2 tablespoons good-quality balsamic vinegar
4 ahi tuna steaks, 6 oz (185 g) each and ¾–1 inch (2–2.5 cm) thick
chopped fresh parsley

Place a large, heavy nonstick frying pan or sauté pan over medium-high heat. When hot, add 1 tablespoon of the olive oil. Add the onion and sprinkle with the sugar. Reduce the heat to medium and sauté, stirring, until lightly browned and soft, about 10 minutes. Season lightly with salt and pepper.

Add the red wine vinegar and cook until most of the liquid evaporates, 1–2 minutes. Add the balsamic vinegar and cook for 30 seconds longer. Transfer the onions to a bowl; cover to keep warm.

Carefully wipe the pan with paper towels and place over medium-high heat. When hot, add the remaining 1 tablespoon oil and heat until very hot but not smoking. Add the tuna steaks and cook until seared on the outside and rare on the inside (see top photo), 1½–2 minutes. Test the fish for doneness (see bottom photo), then season lightly with salt and pepper and transfer to warmed plates. Spoon the onion mixture evenly over each tuna steak, garnish with parsley and serve at once.

Serves 4

POACHING THE FISH
Simmer the fish under at least 2 inches (5 cm) of liquid.

TESTING FOR DONENESS
Use the slotted spatula to lift the fish from the liquid. With a small knife, cut into it along the grain. It should be opaque at the center.

Poached Salmon Steaks with Mustard Sauce

Salmon is particularly delicious when lightly poached in the vegetable-wine stock known as court bouillon, and served with a piquant sauce.

1 cup (8 fl oz/250 ml) dry white
  wine
5 cups (40 fl oz/1.25 l) water
1 small yellow onion, sliced
1 celery stalk, cut into 3 pieces
3 large fresh parsley sprigs
1 bay leaf
6 peppercorns
¼ teaspoon salt
4 salmon steaks, 6 oz (185 g)
  each

FOR THE MUSTARD SAUCE:
2 tablespoons Dijon mustard
2 teaspoons sugar
2 tablespoons red wine vinegar
¼ cup (2 fl oz/60 ml) mild
  vegetable oil
¼ cup (2 oz/60 g) plain low-fat
  yogurt
2 tablespoons chopped fresh
  dill
salt and ground white pepper

*I*n a large sauté pan, combine the wine, water, onion, celery, parsley, bay leaf, peppercorns and salt. Bring to a simmer over medium-low heat and simmer, uncovered, for 20 minutes to blend the flavors.

Meanwhile, to ensure even cooking, secure the ends of the steaks by curling one around the other and piercing with a small skewer.

To make the sauce, in a small bowl, combine the mustard, sugar and vinegar and stir to dissolve the sugar. Gradually whisk in the oil until a thick emulsion forms. Stir in the yogurt and dill and season to taste with salt and white pepper.

Using a slotted spatula, carefully lower the salmon steaks into the simmering liquid. Poach gently (see top photo) until the fish loses its translucency and flakes easily with a fork or the tip of a knife (see bottom photo), 8–10 minutes.

Using the slotted spatula, transfer the steaks to warmed plates. Remove the skewers and pass the mustard sauce at the table.

Serves 4

CLEANING MUSSELS

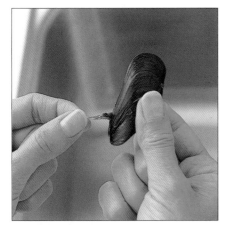

1. PULLING OFF THE BEARDS
Using your fingers, firmly grasp and pull off the tough, fibrous "beard" attached to the hinge of each mussel's shell.

2. SCRUBBING THE SHELLS
Holding mussels under cold running water, use a stiff-bristled brush to scrub the shell, removing any mud, sand or barnacles.

Steamed Mussels with White Wine–Cream Sauce

These delicious but inexpensive mollusks are exceptionally good steamed with white wine and fresh herbs and finished with cream. Serve with crusty French bread and a dry white wine as a first course.

48 mussels in the shell, about
  2 lb (1 kg)
2 shallots, chopped
6 fresh parsley sprigs, plus
  2 tablespoons chopped
  fresh parsley for garnish

3 fresh thyme sprigs
freshly ground pepper
1 cup (8 fl oz/250 ml) dry
  white wine
½ cup (4 fl oz/125 ml) heavy
  (double) cream

*P*ull off the wiry "beards" that are trapped in the shells' hinges and are used for clinging to rocks or pilings (Step 1). Scrub the mussels well (Step 2) and discard any that do not close tightly when touched.

In a large sauté pan, combine the mussels, shallots, parsley and thyme sprigs, a generous sprinkling of pepper and the wine. Place the pan over medium-high heat, cover and cook, shaking the pan occasionally, until the mussels open, about 5 minutes.

Using a slotted spoon, transfer the mussels to warmed shallow soup bowls and cover lightly with aluminum foil to keep warm. Discard any mussels that did not open.

Line a sieve with several thicknesses of cheesecloth (muslin) and strain the cooking liquid through it into a bowl. Return the liquid to the pan, add the cream and boil rapidly over high heat to reduce slightly, about 3 minutes. Pour the reduced sauce over the mussels and sprinkle with the chopped parsley. Serve immediately.

Serves 4

PEELING OFF THE SHELL
With your thumbs, split open the shrimp's shell on its concave side between its two rows of legs and then peel it away.

DEVEINING THE SHRIMP
Using your fingers or the tip of a small knife, pull out the veinlike intestinal tract from along the slit shrimp back.

Baked Shrimp with Fresh Herbs

Delicately flavored shrimp should be cooked quickly so that they remain firm and juicy. One pound (500 g) of large shrimp in the shell, with tails but without heads, will yield just over ½ pound (250 g) of meat. Serve with crusty French bread for sopping up the juices.

2 lb (1 kg) large shrimp (prawns)	2 tablespoons chopped fresh parsley
3 tablespoons olive oil	2 shallots or garlic cloves, finely chopped
1 tablespoon chopped fresh thyme or marjoram	salt and freshly ground pepper

Peel the shrimp (see top photo), leaving the last shell segment intact. Using a small, sharp knife, cut a shallow slit along the back of the shrimp and then remove the vein (see bottom photo). Butterfly the shrimp by cutting deeper into the slit along the shrimp back so that the shrimp can be opened to lay flat; do not cut all the way through. Rinse the shrimp and pat dry.

Grease a large, shallow baking dish with some of the olive oil. Arrange the shrimp in the dish in a single layer, tails upward. In a small bowl, stir together the thyme or marjoram, parsley and shallots or garlic and sprinkle over the shrimp. Season to taste with salt and pepper and drizzle with the remaining olive oil. Cover with plastic wrap and let marinate at cool room temperature for 30 minutes or in the refrigerator for several hours. (Bring to room temperature before baking.)

Preheat an oven to 400°F (200°C). Bake until the shrimp have turned pink and the juices are bubbly, about 8 minutes. Transfer to warmed plates and spoon the pan juices over the top. Serve hot.

Serves 4

HEATING THE OIL IN A HOT WOK
Once the wok (or sauté pan) is very hot, add the oil. It should immediately spread out in ripples to coat the pan.

STIR-FRYING
Using a wok spatula or similar tool, toss and stir the contents, keeping them moving constantly around the bottom and sides.

Stir-fried Scallops with Ginger

Scallops, like oysters or mussels, are bivalve mollusks but, unlike them, are nearly always sold out of the shell in the United States. Scallops should be cooked very briefly, just until they turn opaque.

1 lb (500 g) sea scallops
1 teaspoon cornstarch
1 teaspoon soy sauce
2 teaspoons dry sherry
2 tablespoons peeled and
  minced fresh ginger
1 clove garlic, minced

FOR THE SAUCE:
½ cup (4 fl oz/125 ml) bottled
  clam juice
2 teaspoons cornstarch
  (cornflour)

2 teaspoons water
2 tablespoons soy sauce
½ teaspoon sugar

2 tablespoons mild vegetable
  oil
1 cup (3 oz/90 g) thinly sliced
  green onions
salt
freshly ground pepper
steamed white rice (*recipe on page 32*)

Rinse the scallops and pat dry with paper towels. Cut any large scallops in half horizontally. In a bowl, combine the cornstarch, soy sauce, sherry, ginger and garlic. Add the scallops, toss to coat well and let marinate for 15 minutes.

Meanwhile, make the sauce: In a bowl, combine the clam juice, cornstarch, water, soy sauce and sugar. Stir well and set aside.

Heat a wok or a wide, heavy-bottomed sauté pan over high heat. When hot, add 1 tablespoon of the oil (see top photo). Add the green onions and stir-fry for 30 seconds (see bottom photo). Season lightly with salt. Add the remaining 1 tablespoon oil to the pan, then add the scallops with their marinade and stir-fry for 1 minute. Stir the reserved sauce, add to the pan and stir-fry until the sauce thickens and clears, about 1 minute. Season to taste with pepper. Serve at once with steamed rice.

Serves 4

POULTRY ROASTING BASICS

BEGINNING TO ROAST
To keep the breast meat moist, start the bird breast-side down in the pan.

TURNING AND BASTING
About halfway through roasting, turn the bird breast-side up, baste generously, and continue to roast, basting frequently with the pan juices.

TESTING FOR DONENESS
Prick the thick part of the thigh with a fork or knife: Juices should run clear. Or test with an instant-read thermometer.

Roast Chicken with Gravy

1 chicken, 3½–4 lb (1.75–2 kg)
salt and freshly ground pepper
2 bunches fresh thyme
1 tablespoon unsalted butter, at
  room temperature

1 yellow onion, quartered
2 cups (16 fl oz/500 ml) chicken
  stock (*recipe on page 21*)

Preheat an oven to 375°F (190°C). Remove the giblets from the chicken. Reserve the liver for another use; chop the remaining giblets and reserve for the gravy. Discard any loose fat from around the cavity. Rinse the chicken, pat dry with paper towels and sprinkle inside the chicken cavity and over the surface of the chicken with salt and pepper. Strip enough leaves from 1 bunch of thyme to measure 1 tablespoon and reserve for the gravy. Place the remaining thyme from the bunch in the cavity. Truss the chicken (see page 52). Rub the skin with the butter.

Place the bird in a roasting pan, breast-side down (see top photo). Roast for 30 minutes, basting frequently with the pan juices after the first 10 minutes. Turn breast-side up, baste (see center photo) and add the onion to the pan. Continue to roast, basting frequently, until done, about 30 minutes longer. To test, prick the thigh with a fork (see bottom photo), or insert an instant-read thermometer in the thickest part of the breast or thigh away from the bone; it should read 185°F (85°C) in the thigh, and 170°F (77°C) in the breast.

While the chicken is roasting, in a small saucepan, combine the chicken stock and chopped giblets and bring to a boil. Reduce the heat to low, cover and simmer for 30 minutes. Strain and set aside.

Transfer the chicken to a platter and cover with aluminum foil to keep warm. Make the gravy (see page 11), discarding the onion before pouring off the fat from the roasting pan.

Garnish the chicken with the remaining thyme bunch. Carve at the table and pass the gravy alongside.

Serves 4

1. TYING THE LEGS TOGETHER
With the middle of a long piece of kitchen string, tie together the legs. Bring the string down opposite sides, running it between the thighs and body.

2. SECURING THE WINGS
Flip the chicken over and bring each string end across a wing. Tie at the back to secure the wings against the body.

King Henri's Chicken in a Pot

This is a modern version of poule au pot, *the dish that French King Henri of Navarre wished that all his subjects might enjoy on Sundays.*

1 chicken, about 4 lb (2 kg)	3 or 4 fresh thyme sprigs
½-lb (250-g) piece knuckle or shin of veal	1 bay leaf
	salt, optional
6 cups (48 fl oz/1.5 l) chicken stock (*recipe on page 21*)	16 baby carrots, unpeeled
	2 turnips, peeled and cut lengthwise into eighths
2 carrots, each cut into 4 pieces	
1 yellow onion, quartered	½ small head green cabbage, cored and quartered
1 celery stalk, cut into 4 pieces	
10 peppercorns	2 tablespoons chopped fresh parsley

Remove any giblets from the chicken cavity; set aside for another use. Discard any loose fat from around the cavity. Rinse the chicken, pat dry with paper towels and truss (Steps 1 and 2).

Place the chicken and veal bone in a large pot. Add water to cover, bring to a boil, reduce the heat and simmer for 5 minutes. Remove the chicken and veal, discard the water and rinse the pot.

Add the stock to the pot and bring to a boil. Return the chicken, breast side up, and veal to the pot. Add the carrots, onion, celery, peppercorns, thyme and bay leaf. Cover, return to a boil, reduce the heat to low and simmer gently until an instant-read thermometer inserted into the breast registers 170°F (77°C) or the juices run clear when the thigh is pricked, about 1 hour.

Transfer the chicken to a plate. Strain the broth through a fine-mesh sieve into a bowl. Using a large spoon, skim off the fat from the broth. Rinse the pot and return the broth to it. Add the baby carrots, turnips and cabbage and bring to a boil. Reduce the heat to low and simmer gently until the vegetables are tender, 10–15 minutes.

Discard the string. Carve the chicken and divide it and the vegetables among shallow bowls. Sprinkle with the parsley and serve.

Serves 4

TURNING WITH TONGS
When the top sides have browned, using tongs (to prevent piercing the flesh and releasing the juices), turn the chicken skin-side up.

BASTING WITH A BRUSH
During cooking, use a brush to baste the chicken—in this case, with butter—to keep it moist and promote browning.

Broiled Chicken with Oranges and Watercress

A little-known secret to serving chicken legs successfully is to chop off the knobby drumstick joint. This severs the tough tendon, making the meat easy to cut off the bone once cooked.

¼ cup (2 oz/60 g) unsalted butter	salt
4 whole chicken legs with thigh attached	2 navel or large Valencia oranges
½ lemon	1 large bunch watercress, stemmed, carefully washed and well dried

*P*reheat a broiler (griller). Line a broiler pan with aluminum foil.

In a small saucepan over low heat, melt the butter. Remove from the heat and set aside. Rinse the chicken legs and pat dry with paper towels. Using a meat cleaver or a large chef's knife, chop the end joint off the drumsticks. Rub the legs with the cut lemon and brush generously with some of the melted butter. Sprinkle lightly with salt.

Arrange the chicken legs, skin side down, on the prepared pan and place 5–6 inches (13–15 cm) from the heat. Broil for 10–12 minutes, then turn skin-side up (see top photo). Continue to broil, brushing often with the remaining butter (see bottom photo), until the skin is crisp and golden and juices run clear when the thickest part of the thigh is pricked, about 10 minutes longer.

Meanwhile, use a vegetable peeler to remove the zest in wide strips from half of one of the oranges. Cut the zest into thin slivers. Bring a small saucepan three-fourths full of water to a boil and add the zest strips. Boil for 2 minutes, then drain and set aside. Remove the peel and cut the oranges into segments (see page 25).

Arrange the chicken legs on a warmed platter and garnish with the orange zest slivers, orange segments and watercress.

Serves 4

FLATTENING A BREAST
Place a boneless breast between sheets of
plastic wrap and, using a rolling pin, roll
over the thickest part to make the breast
uniformly thick.

COATING A BREAST
After dusting lightly with flour, first dip in
egg, then in the nut mixture, coating evenly.

Almond-Crusted Chicken Breasts

*Flattening boneless raw chicken breasts to a uniform thickness ensures
that they will cook evenly, retaining their succulence. For a crisp crust,
dip the chicken breast meat into flour, egg and nuts just before cooking.*

4 skinless, boneless chicken
    breast halves, about 6 oz
    (185 g) each
1 egg
salt and freshly ground pepper
½ cup (2 oz/60 g) freshly
    grated Parmesan cheese
½ cup (2 oz/60 g) sliced
    almonds, minced
6 tablespoons unsalted butter,
    at room temperature

3 tablespoons olive oil
all-purpose (plain) flour for
    dusting
2 tablespoons finely chopped
    shallots
4 tablespoons chopped fresh
    parsley
¼ cup (2 fl oz/60 ml) dry white
    wine
lemon wedges

*F*latten each breast to an even ½-inch (12-mm) thickness (see top
photo). In a shallow bowl, lightly beat the egg and season with salt
and pepper. In another bowl, mix the Parmesan and almonds.

In a large frying pan over medium heat, melt 2 tablespoons of
the butter with the olive oil. Dust the chicken breasts with flour,
then dip in the egg, and then in the Parmesan-almond mixture
(see bottom photo). Place the breasts in the pan and cook, turning
once, until golden brown, about 3 minutes total. Using tongs,
transfer to a warmed platter, season lightly with salt and pepper
and keep warm.

Pour off all but a light film of fat from the pan. Place over
medium heat, add the shallots and parsley and sauté, stirring, for
30 seconds. Add the wine and gradually whisk in the remaining
4 tablespoons butter to form a creamy emulsion. Season to taste
with salt and pepper. Spoon the sauce over the chicken breasts
and garnish with lemon wedges. Serve immediately.

Serves 4

FRYING THE MEAT
Place the steaks in the hot pan and fry until browned on the first side. Then turn and fry until browned on the second side.

DEGLAZING THE PAN
Pour the liquid into the hot pan and stir briskly to scrape up browned bits and coagulated juices from the pan bottom.

Filet Mignon with Wine Sauce

There are two secrets to successful panfrying: the meat must be at room temperature, and the frying pan must be a thick and heavy one, as the steaks will stick and scorch in a thin-bottomed pan. An enameled cast-iron pan is a good choice because the meat will cook evenly and the material won't react with the wine to produce an off taste.

4 filet mignon steaks, 6 oz (185 g) each and 1 inch (2.5 cm) thick
1 tablespoon olive oil
salt and freshly ground pepper
½ cup (4 fl oz/125 ml) good-quality red wine

2 tablespoons unsalted butter, at room temperature, cut into pieces
1 small bunch watercress, trimmed, carefully washed and well dried

*T*rim off any fat from the steaks. Pat the steaks dry with paper towels.

Place a heavy frying pan over medium-high heat. When the pan is hot, add the olive oil and heat until hot but not smoking. Add the steaks and fry until evenly browned (see top photo), 6–8 minutes total. When small beads of red juice appear on the surface, the meat is cooked medium-rare. Transfer the steaks to a warmed plate, season to taste with salt and pepper and cover with aluminum foil to keep warm. They will continue to cook for a few seconds longer and the juices will settle.

Add the wine to the frying pan over high heat, stirring to deglaze the pan (see bottom photo). Bring to a boil and boil until reduced to about ¼ cup (2 fl oz/60 ml). Remove from the heat and whisk in the butter. Taste and adjust the seasonings.

Place the steaks on warmed individual plates and pour the sauce over the top. Garnish with the watercress and serve at once.

Serves 4

BROWNING TECHNIQUES

BROWNING CUBES OF MEAT
Working in batches to prevent overcrowding, brown the meat to seal in the juices, turning to color evenly.

BROWNING ONION
Browning the onion in meat juices serves to mellow the onion's acidity and bring out its natural sweetness, as well as to meld the flavor of onion with that of the meat.

Pork Ragout with Polenta

For pork stews and ragouts, use shoulder, blade-end loin or boneless country-style ribs, all of which become tender with long cooking.

2½ lb (1.1 kg) boneless pork (*see note*)
1–2 tablespoons olive oil
1 large yellow onion, halved and sliced
4 cloves garlic, chopped
¼ cup (2 fl oz/60 ml) balsamic vinegar
salt
2 carrots, peeled and diced
1 bay leaf

1½–2 cups (12–16 fl oz/ 375–500 ml) dry red wine
¾–1 cup (6–8 fl oz/180–250 ml) chicken stock (*recipe on page 21*)
hot, soft-cooked polenta (*recipe on page 36*)
½ cup (2½ oz/75 g) drained, oil-packed sun-dried tomatoes, chopped
chopped fresh parsley

Cut the pork into 1½-inch (4-cm) cubes, trimming off any excess fat. Place a large frying pan or sauté pan over medium-high heat. When hot, add 1 tablespoon of the olive oil. When the oil is hot, add the pork and brown evenly (see top photo), about 6 minutes. Transfer the pork to a heavy saucepan.

Add the remaining 1 tablespoon oil, if needed, to the frying pan or sauté pan and place over medium heat. Add the onion and sauté, stirring, until browned (see bottom photo), about 5 minutes, adding the garlic during the last 30 seconds. Stir in the vinegar, scraping up any browned bits from the pan bottom. Pour over the pork and season with salt. Add the carrots, bay leaf, wine and stock almost to cover. Bring to a boil, reduce the heat to low, cover and simmer until the meat is tender, about 1½ hours. About 30 minutes before the pork is done, cook the polenta.

About 15 minutes before the pork is done, stir in the tomatoes and adjust the seasonings. Spoon polenta onto warmed individual plates and top with ragout. Sprinkle with parsley and serve.

Serves 6

BROWNING THE ROAST
Place the flour-dusted roast in the hot pot and brown, turning with metal tongs, to seal in the juices.

TESTING FOR DONENESS
Cover and simmer the meat in a small amount of liquid until a fork inserted into the roast pierces it easily.

Pot-Roasted Top Sirloin

To ensure a succulent finish, pot-roasted beef must be cooked at a gentle simmer; boiling toughens the meat fibers. Use an enameled cast-iron, anodized aluminum or other cladded metal pot with a tight-fitting lid, such as a dutch oven.

½ cup (4 fl oz/125 ml) red wine
3 orange zest strips, each
   3 inches (7.5 cm) long by
   1 inch (2.5 cm) wide
1 small yellow onion, sliced
2 cloves garlic, halved
1 teaspoon salt
6 peppercorns

2 garlic cloves
½ teaspoon dried thyme
all-purpose (plain) flour for
   rubbing on roast
1 top sirloin beef roast, about
   5 lb (2.5 kg)
2 tablespoons unsalted butter
1 tablespoon olive oil

In a small bowl, combine the wine, orange zest, onion, garlic, salt, peppercorns, cloves and thyme. Stir well and set aside.

Rub flour over the roast. In a heavy pot (see note) over medium heat, melt the butter with the oil. When hot, add the roast and brown evenly on all sides (see top photo), about 10 minutes.

Remove the roast and pour off all but a light film of fat from the pot bottom and place the pot over high heat. When hot, pour in the wine mixture and deglaze the pan, stirring to scrape up any browned bits from the pot bottom (see page 58). Return the meat to the pot and turn to coat with the juices. Bring to a boil, reduce the heat to low, cover and simmer gently until the meat tests done (see bottom photo), about 1½ hours longer.

Transfer the meat to a platter and cover to keep warm. Strain the pan juices through a fine-mesh sieve into a small bowl and freeze for a few minutes until the fat rises to the surface. Skim off the fat and discard. Reheat the juices and pour into a serving dish.

Slice the meat across the grain (see Slicing Meat, page 11) and arrange on the platter. Pass the juices at the table.

Serves 10

BROWNING THE CHOPS
Heat a cast-iron or other heavy ovenproof frying pan over high heat. When hot, add the chops and sear on the first side. Using tongs so as not to pierce the meat, turn and sear on the second side.

FINISHING IN THE OVEN
Season the seared chops—here, with rosemary—before placing in the preheated oven to finish cooking.

Lamb Chops with Herb Butter

By searing the lamb chops on the stove top first and then finishing them in the oven, they cook to a perfect and juicy medium-rare.

1 large clove garlic, unpeeled	1 tablespoon fresh rosemary
1 tablespoon olive oil	salt and freshly ground pepper
4 loin lamb chops, trimmed of fat and 1½ inches (4 cm) thick	2 tablespoons unsalted butter
	1 tablespoon finely chopped fresh parsley

Preheat an oven to 400°F (200°C).

Cut the garlic clove in half crosswise and rub the cut surfaces over a large, rimmed plate. Pour the olive oil onto the plate. Place the chops on the oil, turning to coat well.

Place a heavy ovenproof frying pan over high heat. When hot, add the chops and brown evenly to seal in the juices (see top photo), about 1 minute on the first side and 30 seconds on the second side. Sprinkle the tops of the chops with the rosemary and place the pan in the oven (see bottom photo).

Bake until medium-rare, about 8 minutes. To test for doneness, press gently on the meat with your finger; the meat should feel springy, much like your palm at the base of your thumb. Transfer the chops to warmed individual plates. Season to taste with salt and pepper.

Add the butter to the pan over high heat and stir to scrape up any browned bits from the pan bottom. Stir in the parsley. Spoon the sauce over the chops. Serve immediately.

Serves 2

POACHING FRESH ASPARAGUS

PEELING THE SPEARS
After removing the tough, woody ends, peel off the thin skin covering the spears, peeling about two-thirds of each spear.

POACHING THE SPEARS
Add the asparagus to a frying pan half-filled with simmering water and poach until bright green and tender-crisp when pierced with a knife.

Poached Asparagus

Asparagus is at its best in April and May. Look for firm, bright green spears with tightly furled tips. Removing the tough end and peeling the fibrous, green outer layer of each spear before cooking yields an especially tender result.

24 medium-large asparagus spears	3 tablespoons unsalted butter, melted
salt	¼ cup (2 oz/60 g) freshly grated Parmesan cheese

Cut or snap off any tough, woody ends from the asparagus spears and discard. Using a vegetable peeler and starting about 2 inches (5 cm) below the tip, peel off the skin from each spear (see top photo).

Select a sauté pan large enough to hold the spears flat in a single layer and half fill with water. Bring to a boil, then reduce the heat so the water simmers gently with just a few bubbles breaking on the surface. Lay the asparagus spears flat in the pan so they are covered with about 1 inch (2.5 cm) of water and poach until tender-crisp (see bottom photo), 5–8 minutes. Begin testing with a knife tip after 4 minutes; the timing will depend upon the thickness of the spears.

Remove from the heat and drain well. Arrange the spears on a warmed serving dish. Season lightly with salt and drizzle the tips with the melted butter. Sprinkle with the cheese and serve.

Serves 4

BRUSHING MUSHROOMS CLEAN
Using a mushroom brush, brush the dirt from the mushrooms. Alternatively, wipe clean with damp paper towels.

SAUTÉING THE MUSHROOMS
Sauté the mushrooms over medium heat, adjusting heat if necessary. If too high, the mushrooms will burn; if too low, they will exude juice and steam instead of fry.

Garlic Mushrooms

Serve this appetizing mushroom mixture as a first course with crusty bread; as a side dish or sauce with beef steaks, lamb chops or chicken; as a topping for polenta (recipe on page 36); or as a pasta sauce. Use a mixture of fresh mushroom varieties, if possible.

1 lb (500 g) fresh mushrooms such as cremini, portobello or shiitake, in any combination
¼ cup (2 oz/60 g) unsalted butter
2 tablespoons olive oil
2 tablespoons minced shallots
1 tablespoon minced garlic
2 tablespoons minced fresh parsley
½ cup (4 fl oz/125 ml) chicken stock *(recipe on page 21)*
salt and freshly ground pepper

*B*rush the mushrooms clean with a mushroom brush (see top photo) or damp paper towels; do not rinse them in water, as they will absorb too much moisture. Trim off and discard the stems, then slice the mushrooms vertically ¼ inch (6 mm) thick.

In a large frying pan or sauté pan over medium heat, melt the butter with the olive oil. Add the shallots and garlic and sauté, stirring, until softened, about 3 minutes. Add the mushrooms and sauté, stirring, until glossy and golden (see bottom photo), about 8 minutes.

Add the parsley and chicken stock, stir well and cook for 2 minutes longer. Season to taste with salt and pepper and serve.

Serves 4

PEELING PEARL ONIONS

1. TRIMMING AND CUTTING AN X
Cut the root end from each blanched onion. Then, cut a small, shallow X in the root end to prevent the onion from telescoping as it cooks.

2. SLIPPING OFF THE SKINS
Grasp the stem end of an onion between thumb and forefinger and squeeze gently to slip off the skin.

Sautéed Pearl Onions

Based on a classic recipe from northern Italy, these delicious little onions are a complementary side dish to poultry or meat. Not to be mistaken for the slightly larger white boiling onions, pearl onions are about ¾ inch (2 cm) in diameter and are often sold in small baskets that each hold about ⅔ pound (315 g). Blanching the onions in boiling water, then refreshing them in cold water effectively loosens the skins, making them easier to peel.

1¼ lb (625 g) pearl onions
1 tablespoon unsalted butter
1 tablespoon olive oil
1 small bay leaf
2 fresh oregano sprigs

⅔ cup (5 fl oz/160 ml) chicken stock *(recipe on page 21)*
salt and white pepper
⅔ cup (5 fl oz/160 ml) dry white wine

*F*ill a saucepan three-fourths full with water and bring to a boil over high heat. Add the onions and blanch for 2 minutes. Drain, plunge into cold water to cool and drain again. Using a sharp knife, cut off the root end from each onion and then cut a small, shallow X in the end (Step 1). Slip off the skins (Step 2) and cut off the long stem tails, if necessary.

In a heavy frying pan over medium-low heat, melt the butter with the olive oil. When hot, add the onions, bay leaf, oregano sprigs, chicken stock, and salt and white pepper to taste. Cook gently, stirring occasionally, until the stock evaporates and the onions start to brown, about 10 minutes. Add the wine and continue to cook, shaking the pan often to turn the onions, until the sauce reduces to a syrupy glaze, about 2 minutes.

Discard the bay leaf and oregano sprigs and serve at once.

Serves 4

PREPARING & STEAMING FRESH BROCCOLI

PEELING THE STALKS
Peel the stalks of their tough, fibrous outer layer before cutting them into thick slices.

STEAMING FRESH BROCCOLI
Steam the broccoli in a steamer basket—shown here—or steamer insert set over boiling water until tender, but not mushy.

Steamed Broccoli with Pine Nuts

Broccoli is available year-round, but is at its best from autumn through spring. Look for compact, tightly furled buds, relatively slender stalks and a deep green color. When cooked, it should be firm to the bite.

2 tablespoons pine nuts
1½ lb (750 g) broccoli

2 tablespoons unsalted butter, melted
salt

*I*n a small frying pan over medium-low heat, toast the pine nuts, shaking the pan often, until golden and fragrant, 2–3 minutes. Set aside.

Trim the ends of the broccoli stalks and cut off any coarse outer leaves. Cut off the flower heads and then divide the heads into florets with short stems; cut any large florets in half. Using a vegetable peeler, peel the thick stalks to reveal their pale green flesh (see top photo). Using a sharp knife, cut on the diagonal into slices ⅓ inch (9 mm) thick.

Steam the broccoli in a two-part steamer or a collapsible steamer basket and large pot. *If using a two-part steamer,* fill the bottom one-fourth full with water, place over high heat and bring to a boil. Place the broccoli in the perforated top section and set it over the boiling water. *If using a collapsible steamer basket,* arrange the broccoli in the steamer basket set over 1 inch (2.5 cm) of boiling water in a saucepan with a lid (see bottom photo).

Cover and steam until the stalks are just tender when pierced with a knife, about 5 minutes.

Transfer the broccoli to a warmed serving dish and drizzle the melted butter over the top. Toss gently and season lightly with salt. Top with the toasted pine nuts and serve.

Serves 4

GRILLING OUTDOORS ON A CHARCOAL GRILL
Position the rack over hot coals, brush
lightly with oil and arrange the vegetables
on top. Turn as needed to brown evenly.

GRILLING INDOORS ON A GRILL PAN
Heat a ridged grill pan over medium heat.
Arrange the vegetables on it in a single
layer. Turn as needed to brown evenly.

Grilled Vegetables

*Charcoal grills are prized among outdoor cooks for the subtle smoky
flavor they impart to food. But for those who want grill cooking without
having to build a charcoal fire, a ridged grill pan is a good alternative.*

2 small zucchini (courgettes)
2 slender (Asian) eggplants
  (aubergines)
1 fennel bulb
4 tablespoons (2 fl oz/60 ml)
  olive oil, plus oil for rack

2 teaspoons dried herbes de
  Provence
salt and freshly ground pepper

Trim off the ends of the zucchini and eggplants. Cut each zucchini
lengthwise into 3 strips, and cut each eggplant in half lengthwise.
Discard the feathery tops and stalks from the fennel bulb. Cut away
any discolored areas, then cut the bulb lengthwise into quarters
with the core intact. Bring a small saucepan three-fourths full of
water to a boil. Add the fennel, reduce the heat to medium-low
and simmer until just tender, 15–20 minutes. Drain and set aside.

  Pour 3 tablespoons of the olive oil onto a deep platter and
sprinkle with the herbs. Add the vegetables and turn to coat.

  To cook on a charcoal grill, mound the coals and light them.
When the coals are edged with gray ash, spread them out and
position the grill rack 4–6 inches (10–15 cm) above the heat.

  To cook on a ridged grill pan, heat the pan over medium heat
until hot.

  Lay the vegetables on the grill rack or pan and grill, turning
once, until tender and marked with golden brown grill marks
(see techniques at left), 3–4 minutes per side.

  Transfer the vegetables to warmed plates. Season with salt and
pepper. Drizzle with the remaining 1 tablespoon oil and serve.

Serves 4 as a first course, 2 as a main course

BEATING EGG WHITES
In a bowl, preferably of unlined copper, use a balloon whisk to beat egg whites until stiff enough to hold soft, moist peaks.

FOLDING EGG WHITES INTO SAUCE
Using a rubber spatula, stir about one-fourth of the whites into the cheese sauce. Fold in the remaining whites by cutting down, underneath and over them.

Classic Cheese Soufflé

For the maximum volume in a soufflé, the egg whites must be beaten to soft (not stiff) peaks and then evenly folded into the soufflé base.

3 tablespoons unsalted butter
4 tablespoons (1 oz/30 g) freshly grated good-quality Parmesan cheese
2 tablespoons all-purpose (plain) flour
1 cup (8 fl oz/250 ml) milk, heated

1 cup (4 oz/125 g) shredded Gruyère cheese
4 large eggs, at room temperature, separated
salt and ground white pepper
pinch of ground nutmeg

Preheat an oven to 375°F (190°C). Grease a 1-qt (1-l) soufflé dish with 1 tablespoon of the butter and dust with 2 tablespoons of the Parmesan cheese. Set aside.

In a saucepan over low heat, melt the remaining 2 tablespoons butter. Using a wooden spoon, stir in the flour; continue to stir until golden. Whisk in the hot milk, then stir over medium heat until the mixture is thick and smooth. Reduce the heat to low and simmer, stirring constantly, until very thick, 3–4 minutes. Remove from the heat; stir in the Gruyère cheese and the remaining 2 table-spoons Parmesan until melted. In a small bowl, lightly beat the egg yolks. Beat 3 tablespoons of the hot cheese mixture into the yolks, then gradually beat the yolk mixture into the cheese mixture. Season lightly with salt and pepper and the nutmeg. Set aside.

In a large bowl, using a balloon whisk or an electric mixer, beat the egg whites to soft peaks (see top photo). Stir one-fourth of the whites into the cheese sauce to lighten it then, working in 2 or 3 more batches, add the remaining whites and quickly fold them in (see bottom photo). Spoon into the prepared dish.

Bake until well risen, golden brown and a skewer inserted into the center comes out moist, about 25 minutes. Serve at once.

Serves 4

SLIPPING EGGS INTO SIMMERING WATER
One at a time, break each egg into a saucer. Holding the saucer close to the simmering water, gently slip in the egg.

REMOVING AND TRIMMING THE EGGS
When the whites are set and the yolks glazed, lift out the eggs with a slotted spoon and trim the ragged edges with a knife.

Poached Eggs in Chard Nests

A little vinegar added to the poaching water helps to coagulate the egg whites. You can cook the eggs in advance and store them in a bowl of water; reheat in a pan of simmering water before serving.

2 lb (1 kg) Swiss chard	½ cup (4 fl oz/125 ml) water
4 tablespoons (2 oz/60 g) unsalted butter	salt and freshly ground pepper
2 tablespoons olive oil	1 teaspoon white wine vinegar
	4 eggs, at room temperature

Cut the center stems from the chard leaves. Keeping the stems separate from the leaves, rinse well and drain. Cut the stems crosswise into thin slices; chop the leaves coarsely.

In a large frying pan over medium-low heat, melt half of the butter with the olive oil. Add the stems and sauté, stirring, for 5 minutes. Add the leaves and continue to sauté, stirring often, until wilted, about 2 minutes longer. Add the water and a pinch of salt, cover, reduce the heat to low and simmer until tender, 10–15 minutes. Drain the chard and return it to the pan. Season to taste with salt and pepper. Cover to keep warm.

Meanwhile, half fill a nonstick 12-inch (30-cm) sauté pan with water. Add the vinegar and ½ teaspoon salt and bring the water to a simmer over high heat. Reduce the heat to low to maintain a gentle simmer. Using a saucer, slip 1 egg at a time into the water (see top photo). When the whites have firmed up slightly, spoon the barely simmering water over the eggs and continue to cook until the whites are set, milky looking and opaque and the yolks are just glazed but still soft, 2–3 minutes.

Meanwhile, cut the remaining butter into small bits and stir into the chard, tossing to coat evenly. Divide among 4 warmed plates and make a nest in the center of each mound.

Remove the eggs from the water and trim the untidy edges (see bottom photo). Place an egg in each chard nest and serve at once.

Serves 4

PREPARING POTATO GRATIN

SLICING WITH A MANDOLINE
A mandoline is ideal for cutting thin, uniform slices. Slide the item to be sliced—here, a potato—up and down the cutting surface. Transfer the slices to a bowl of water.

LAYERING THE POTATOES
After arranging a layer of potatoes on the bottom of the baking dish and sprinkling with cheese, top with another layer, arranging them like shingles on a roof.

French-Style Potato Gratin

This dish is prepared in the style of France's mountainous Savoy region. The potatoes must be very thinly sliced and of even thickness, and then rinsed and dried to rid them of surface starch.

1½ lb (750 g) waxy potatoes such as White Rose, Yukon Gold or a red-skinned variety
1 clove garlic, unpeeled
3 tablespoons unsalted butter, at room temperature
salt and ground white pepper
freshly grated nutmeg
2 oz (60 g) Gruyère cheese, shredded
1¼ cups (10 fl oz/310 ml) chicken stock *(recipe page 21)*

Preheat an oven to 350°F (180°C). Peel the potatoes. Using a mandoline (see top photo), a food processor with the thin slicing disk, or a sharp knife, slice the potatoes ⅛ inch (3 mm) thick. Transfer the slices to a bowl of cold water; let stand for 5 minutes to remove the starch, which can cause the slices to stick together.

Cut the garlic clove in half crosswise and rub the cut sides over the bottom and sides of an 8-by-10-inch (20-by-25-cm) earthenware baking dish; discard the garlic. Grease the dish with 1 tablespoon of the butter. Drain the potato slices and pat dry with paper towels. Arrange half of the potatoes in overlapping rows in the dish. Season to taste with salt and white pepper and a generous sprinkling of nutmeg. Sprinkle with half of the cheese. Cut the remaining 2 tablespoons butter into small pieces and use half of it to dot the surface. Overlap the remaining potato slices in rows on the top (see bottom photo). Pour the stock over the potatoes. Season to taste with salt, white pepper and nutmeg. Top with the remaining cheese and dot with the remaining butter.

Bake, uncovered, until the potatoes are tender when pierced with a fork and the surface is golden, about 1 hour.

Let cool for a few minutes, then serve.

Serves 4

PURÉEING WITH A RICER
A few pieces at a time, put the boiled, unpeeled potato quarters in a ricer held over a bowl. Squeeze the handle to force the potatoes through the holes.

PURÉEING WITH A MASHER
Place the boiled, peeled potatoes in a bowl and press down with a hand-held potato masher, continuing until no lumps remain.

Mashed Potatoes

To be at their best, mashed potatoes must be freshly made and free of lumps. Mashing them in a potato ricer or coarse sieve usually yields the smoothest texture; hand-held mashers are also a good choice, although they require a little more work. There is no need to peel potatoes mashed in a ricer or coarse sieve; the peel is strained out when the boiled potatoes are pressed through the small holes.

4 baking potatoes, about 2 lb (1 kg) total weight
salt
½ cup (4 fl oz/125 ml) whole or low-fat milk, or as needed
¼ cup (2 oz/60 g) unsalted butter, or as needed
ground white pepper

*I*f mashing with a potato masher, peel the potatoes. Cut the peeled or unpeeled potatoes into quarters and place in a saucepan. Add cold water to cover and a pinch of salt and bring to a boil. Reduce the heat to medium and simmer briskly, uncovered, until tender when pierced with a fork, about 20 minutes.

Drain the potatoes and return to the pan. Place over low heat and stir for 1 minute to dry out completely. Mash the potatoes in a ricer (see top photo) or with a hand-held potato masher (see bottom photo), or position a large coarse sieve over a bowl and press the potatoes through with the back of a spoon.

Combine the ½ cup (4 fl oz/125 ml) milk and ¼ cup (2 oz/60 g) butter in the same pan in which the potatoes were cooked and place over medium-low heat. When the butter melts and the mixture is warm, add the potatoes. Using a wooden spoon, beat hard to incorporate the butter and milk fully and form a creamy consistency. Add a little more milk or butter if needed. Season the potatoes to taste with salt and white pepper, transfer to a warmed serving dish and serve hot.

Serves 4

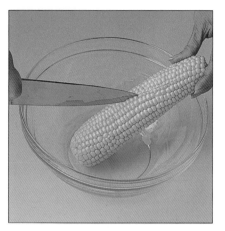

SLITTING CORN KERNELS
Holding an ear of corn in a bowl to capture any juices, use the tip of a knife to slit down the center of each row of corn kernels.

SCRAPING CORN COBS
Using the dull side of the knife, scrape down the corn cob to extract the corn pulp and juices without the skins.

Farmers' Market Corn Custard

Make this delicious side dish when young corn has been freshly picked and is still very sweet; as ears of corn age, the natural sugar in the kernels turns to starch. This custard does not call for eggs, as the milky young corn supplies enough thickening.

1 tablespoon unsalted butter, at room temperature
4 or 5 ears very fresh corn

⅓ cup (3 fl oz/80 ml) heavy (double) cream
salt and freshly ground pepper
pinch of ground nutmeg

Preheat an oven to 375°F (190°C). Grease a shallow 1-qt (1-l) baking dish with the butter. Pull the green husks off the corn, remove the silk filaments and then wipe the ears clean with a paper towel.

Working with 1 ear of corn at a time, place stem-end down in a shallow bowl. Using a sharp, heavy knife, make a lengthwise cut down the center of each row of kernels (see top photo). Then, holding the ear at a 30-degree angle and using the dull side of the knife blade at a 90-degree angle to the ear, carefully scrape all of the pulp out of the kernels (see bottom photo). Repeat with the remaining ears of corn. There should be about 2 cups (12 oz/375 g) of kernels, pulp and juice.

Using a fork, stir the cream into the corn and season to taste with salt, pepper and nutmeg, mixing well. Transfer the mixture to the prepared baking dish. Bake until the custard has thickened and puffed up slightly and the surface is lightly browned, 30–35 minutes. Serve immediately.

Serves 4

PREPARING YEAST DOUGH

KNEADING YEAST DOUGH
On a floured work surface, fold the dough in half toward you, then push it away from you with the heel of your hand. Repeat.

LETTING DOUGH RISE
Place the dough in an oiled bowl, turning to grease all sides. Cover with plastic wrap and let rise until doubled in bulk.

PLACING DOUGH IN PAN
Roll out the dough and place it in the pan. Using your fingertips, pat it out evenly to cover the pan bottom.

Herb and Olive Focaccia

1 package (2¼ teaspoons) quick-rise yeast
1¼ cups (10 fl oz/310 ml) warm water (110°F/43°C)
2 tablespoons olive oil
1 tablespoon chopped fresh oregano, rosemary or sage
1 teaspoon salt
freshly ground pepper
3½–4 cups (17½–20 oz/545–625 g) unbleached bread flour

FOR THE TOPPING:
1 small yellow onion, quartered and sliced
2 tablespoons chopped fresh oregano, rosemary or sage
24 oil-cured black olives, pitted and chopped
1½ tablespoons olive oil, plus oil for greasing pan

*I*n a large bowl, dissolve the yeast in the warm water and let stand until bubbles start to rise, about 5 minutes. Add the oil, the herb of choice, salt and a generous grinding of pepper. Gradually stir in 3 cups (15 oz/470 g) of the flour.

Turn out the dough onto a floured surface and knead (see top photo), adding flour to prevent sticking, until supple and elastic, 10–12 minutes. Place the dough in an oiled bowl, cover and let rise in a warm spot until doubled (see center photo), 45–60 minutes.

Meanwhile, make the topping: Combine the onion, herb of choice, olives and 1 tablespoon of the oil; mix well. Set aside.

Grease a 17-by-11-by-1-inch (43-by-28-by-2.5-cm) rimmed baking sheet with olive oil. Punch down the dough in the bowl and turn out onto a work surface. Cover and let rest for 10 minutes. Using a rolling pin, roll out into a rectangle similar in size to the pan. Transfer the dough to the pan and press it in (see bottom photo). Brush with the remaining ½ tablespoon oil. Cover and let rise until doubled, 30–40 minutes. Preheat an oven to 425°F (220°C).

Using outspread fingertips, make "dimples" over the surface of the dough, spacing them 1 inch (2.5 cm) apart. Sprinkle on the topping and bake until well browned, 18–20 minutes. Let cool in the pan for 5 minutes, then transfer to a rack. Serve warm.

Serves 8

STRETCHING FOR A THIN DOUGH
Drape the flattened dough over the backs of your fists. Being careful not to break through the dough, stretch and turn it to form a large, thin circle that is slightly thicker at the edges.

SPOONING ON THE TOPPING
Spoon the topping evenly over the dough to within 1 inch (2.5 cm) of the edge.

Pizza with Onions and Peppers

1 teaspoon quick-rise yeast
1 cup (8 fl oz/250 ml) warm
water (110°F/43°C)
2½–3 cups (12½–15 oz/
390–470 g) unbleached
bread flour
½ teaspoon salt
olive oil

FOR THE TOPPING:
2 tablespoons olive oil
3 yellow onions, sliced
2 cloves garlic, minced
1 red bell pepper (capsicum),
roasted, peeled (*see page 14*)
and sliced into narrow strips
salt and freshly ground pepper
20 oil-cured olives, halved

In a large bowl, dissolve the yeast in the warm water and let stand until bubbles start to rise, about 5 minutes. Gradually stir in 2 cups (10 oz/315 g) of the flour.

Turn out the dough onto a lightly floured work surface and knead (see top photo, page 87), adding flour as needed to prevent sticking, until smooth, supple and elastic, 10–12 minutes. Gather into a ball, place in an oiled bowl, cover and let rise in a warm spot until doubled, 35–45 minutes (see center photo, page 87).

Turn out the dough onto a lightly floured work surface and press flat. Form into 2 equal balls and dust lightly with flour. Let rest, uncovered, for 5 minutes. Wrap 1 ball and freeze for later use.

Oil a 12-inch (30-cm) pizza pan or baking sheet. Press the dough flat, then shape into a 12-inch (30-cm) round (see top photo). Place on the prepared pan, cover with greased plastic wrap and let rise until puffy, 15–20 minutes. Preheat an oven to 400°F (200°C).

Meanwhile, make the topping: In a frying pan over medium heat, warm the oil. Add the onions and sauté until soft, 6–7 minutes. Add the garlic and bell pepper and sauté until soft, about 3 minutes. Season with salt and pepper. Spoon the topping over the dough (see bottom photo), sprinkle with the olives and bake until golden around the edges, about 20 minutes. Serve hot.

Serves 6–8 as a first course, 2 or 3 as a main course

MIXING LIQUID AND DRY INGREDIENTS
After cutting the butter into the flour mixture, add milk and stir briefly with a fork until the dough clings together.

KNEADING THE DOUGH
Using your palms and the heels of your hands, knead the dough gently 4 or 5 times just until it holds together.

Berry Shortcakes

Always leave tiny lumps of butter in shortcake dough; they melt during baking to create air spaces that help form a flaky structure.

1 cup (5 oz/155 g) all-purpose (plain) flour
2 tablespoons granulated sugar
1 teaspoon baking powder
¼ teaspoon salt
¼ cup (2 oz/60 g) cold unsalted butter, cut into cubes
6 tablespoons (3 fl oz/90 ml) milk

FOR THE BERRY AND CREAM FILLING:

3 cups (12 oz/375 g) mixed fresh berries
5 tablespoons (2 oz/60 g) superfine (castor) sugar
½ cup (4 fl oz/125 ml) heavy (double) cream
1 tablespoon orange liqueur

Preheat an oven to 400°F (200°C). In a bowl, sift together the flour, granulated sugar, baking powder and salt. Cut the butter into the flour (see top photo, page 98). Stir in the milk until the dough clings together (see top photo).

Turn out the mixture onto a lightly floured surface and knead gently (see bottom photo). Lightly form into a ball, transfer to a greased baking sheet and pat into a disk about 7 inches (18 cm) in diameter. Cut into 4 equal wedges. Bake until golden, 12–15 minutes. Let cool on a wire rack.

Meanwhile, make the filling: Place ½ cup (2 oz/60 g) of the berries in a bowl and mash with a fork. Stir in 4 tablespoons (2 oz/ 60 g) of the sugar. Add the remaining berries and stir to mix. In a separate bowl, using an electric mixer on medium-high speed or a wire whisk, beat the cream with the remaining 1 tablespoon sugar and the liqueur just until soft peaks form.

Use a fork to split the shortcakes in half horizontally. Place the bottom halves, cut sides up, on individual plates. Spoon the berries and cream onto the bottoms. Replace the top halves and serve.

Serves 4

POACHING CUT SIDES DOWN
Place the fruit halves in the simmering poaching liquid, arranging them cut sides down and in a single layer.

TURNING THE FRUIT
Using a large slotted spoon and fork, carefully turn the fruit about halfway through cooking, then continue poaching until a toothpick pierces them easily.

Poached Pears with Zabaglione

The slightly grainy texture of the cold, honeyed pears contrasts beautifully with the warm richness of Italy's famed frothy dessert.

4 firm but ripe Comice or
  Bartlett (Williams') pears
1 cup (8 fl oz/250 ml) sweet
  white dessert wine
1 cup (8 fl oz/250 ml) water
½ cup (6 oz/185 g) honey
1 lemon zest strip, 3 inches
  (7.5 cm) long by 1 inch
  (2.5 cm) wide

FOR THE ZABAGLIONE SAUCE:
5 egg yolks, plus 1 whole egg
3 tablespoons sugar
½ cup (4 fl oz/125 ml) Marsala
  wine

¼ cup (2 oz/60 g) mascarpone
  or whipped cream cheese, at
  room temperature
fresh mint sprigs, optional

*P*eel the pears and cut in half lengthwise. Using a small spoon or a melon baller, remove the core from each half to make an even cavity, then cut out the stem. In a wide sauté pan, combine the wine, water, honey and zest. Bring to a boil, stirring often. Reduce the heat to low and simmer for 5 minutes. Add the pear halves, cut sides down (see top photo). Poach, turning once, until tender (see bottom photo), 5–10 minutes. Let the pears cool in the poaching liquid, then cover and refrigerate.

To make the sauce, bring a saucepan half full of water to a simmer. In a stainless-steel or unlined copper bowl, combine the egg yolks, whole egg and sugar. Place the bowl over (not touching) the simmering water. Using a wire whisk or a hand-held electric mixer, beat until pale yellow and fluffy, about 3 minutes. Gradually add the Marsala, beating until the mixture is just thick enough to hold its shape in a spoon, 6–7 minutes. Remove from over the water.

Divide the sauce among 4 dessert bowls. Using a slotted spoon, transfer the pear halves to the bowls, placing 2 halves, cavity sides up, in each. Mound some of the mascarpone or cream cheese in each cavity and garnish with mint sprigs, if desired. Serve at once.

Serves 4

MAKING A GENOISE BATTER

HEATING EGGS AND SUGAR
Beat the egg mixture in a bowl set over simmering water until just warm.

BEATING TO THE RIBBON STAGE
Beat off the heat until the mixture is cool, tripled in volume and falls in a ribbon that slowly dissolves on the surface.

FOLDING IN FLOUR
Gently fold in the sifted flour with a rubber spatula, cutting down to the bottom, up the sides and then bringing the batter over the top to maintain maximum volume.

Lemon Sponge Cake

True sponge cake requires no baking powder or other leavener. Its light texture is derived from air trapped within well-beaten eggs.

unsalted butter for greasing pan
1 small lemon
3 large eggs
6 tablespoons (3 oz/90 g) granulated sugar
¼ teaspoon vanilla extract (essence)
½ cup (2 oz/60 g) plus 2 tablespoons cake (soft-wheat) flour
tiny pinch of salt
confectioners' (icing) sugar

*P*reheat an oven to 350°F (180°C). Butter a cake pan 8 inches (20 cm) in diameter and 2 inches (5 cm) deep, line the bottom with parchment paper, and butter the paper.

Zest the lemon (see page 9). Mince the zest finely and set aside.

Half fill a saucepan with water and bring to a simmer. Meanwhile, place the eggs and sugar in a nonplastic bowl. Beat with an electric mixer set on medium speed or a balloon whisk just until blended. Place the bowl over (not touching) the simmering water and continue beating until the mixture is warm (Step 1), 2–3 minutes. Remove the bowl from the heat and continue beating to the ribbon stage (Step 2), 6–7 minutes. Stir in the vanilla and lemon zest.

Sift the cake flour and salt onto the egg mixture and fold it in (Step 3), giving the bowl a quarter turn with each fold. Pour the batter into the prepared pan and smooth the top.

Bake until the cake feels springy to a light finger touch, 20–25 minutes. Let cool in the pan on a rack for 1 minute, then invert onto the rack and peel off the paper. Let cool completely.

Place the cake, right side up, on a serving plate. Sift confectioners' sugar evenly over the top. Cut into wedges to serve.

Makes one 8-inch (20-cm) cake; serves 6–8

TESTING THE CUSTARD FOR DONENESS
Cook the custard mixture until it is thick enough to coat the back of the spoon. To test, run a finger across it; it should leave a path.

FORMING A CARAMEL TOPPING
Sprinkle a thin, even layer of superfine sugar over the chilled custards, then place under a broiler (griller) until caramelized.

Crème Brûlée

Crème brûlée has a cool, silky-smooth richness that is perfectly complemented by a crisp topping of hot, caramelized sugar.

2 cups (16 fl oz/500 ml) heavy (double) cream
4 egg yolks
2 tablespoons plus ⅓ cup (3 oz/90 g) superfine (castor) sugar

½ teaspoon vanilla extract (essence)
raspberries, blackberries or sliced strawberries (optional)

*I*n a heavy saucepan over medium-low heat, warm the cream until little bubbles form around the edges. Remove from the heat and set aside. In a large, nonplastic bowl, combine the egg yolks and the 2 tablespoons sugar. Using a wire whisk, beat until light in color. Beat in the vanilla. Using a wooden spoon, gradually stir in the warm cream.

Fill a saucepan one-fourth full with water and bring to a simmer over low heat. Set the bowl over (not touching) the water in the pan and cook, stirring, until the custard thickly coats the back of the spoon (see top photo), about 8 minutes.

Pour the custard through a fine-mesh sieve into four 1-cup (8-fl oz/250-ml) ramekins. Sprinkle your choice of berries into the custards, if desired. Let cool, then refrigerate for at least 2 hours or, covered, for up to 24 hours.

Preheat a broiler (griller). Sprinkle the ⅓ cup (3 oz/90 g) sugar over the custards (see bottom photo). Place the ramekins on a baking sheet. Place the sheet under the broiler 5–6 inches (13–15 cm) from the heat source. Broil (grill) until the sugar caramelizes, forming a brittle layer that looks like a brown-and-gold tortoiseshell; this will happen almost immediately. Remove from the broiler and serve at once.

Serves 6

TART PASTRY TECHNIQUES

CUTTING FAT INTO FLOUR
Using a pastry blender (shown here) or
2 knives, cut the butter into the flour
mixture until it resembles fine meal.

STIRRING THE DOUGH TOGETHER
After stirring in the egg, gradually stir
in enough of the cold water to form
a crumbly mass.

LINING THE TART PAN
Roll the dough around the rolling pin,
position it over the pan, then unroll it
and press it gently into the pan.

Plum Tart with Toasted Almonds

FOR THE PASTRY DOUGH:
1 cup (5 oz/155 g) plus 3 table-
    spoons all-purpose (plain)
    flour
1 tablespoon granulated sugar
pinch of salt
½ cup (4 oz/125 g) cold unsalted
    butter, cut into pieces
1 egg, beaten
1–2 tablespoons cold water

FOR THE FILLING:
1 cup (8 oz/250 g) granulated
    sugar
½ cup (4 fl oz/125 ml) water
½ cup (4 fl oz/125 ml) red
    wine
2 lb (1 kg) black or red plums,
    halved and pitted
1 tablespoon brown sugar
1–2 tablespoons sliced almonds,
    toasted

*I*n a bowl, combine the flour, granulated sugar and salt. Add the
butter and cut it into the flour (see top photo). Stir in the egg.
Then stir in enough of the water, 1 teaspoon at a time, to form a
loose mass (see center photo). Form into a ball, wrap well and
chill for 30 minutes.

On a lightly floured surface, roll out the dough into a round
11 inches (28 cm) in diameter, dusting with flour as needed to
prevent sticking. Transfer the dough to a 9-inch (23-cm) tart
pan with a removable bottom (see bottom photo). Turn the over-
hang under and press against the inside edge of the pan to make
a double-thick edge flush with the pan rim. Cover with plastic
wrap and refrigerate for at least 20 minutes or for several hours.

Meanwhile, make the filling: In a wide sauté pan, bring the granulated sugar, water and wine to a boil, stirring. Reduce the heat and
simmer for 5 minutes. Add the plums, cut sides up, and poach
until tender, about 5 minutes. Using a slotted spoon, transfer the
plums, cut sides down, to a rack to drain. Let cool, then peel.

Preheat an oven to 400°F (200°C). Arrange the plums snugly in
the tart shell, cut sides down; sprinkle with the brown sugar. Bake
until the pastry is golden, about 25 minutes. Remove the pan
sides, sprinkle with the almonds and serve warm.

Makes one 8½-inch (21.5-cm) tart; serves 6–8

CREAMING BUTTER AND SUGAR
Using (preferably) the paddle or the whisk attachment, beat the butter and sugar on medium speed until light and fluffy.

BEATING IN THE EGGS
Beat the eggs into the butter-sugar mixture a little at a time, so that the batter emulsifies and does not separate.

Orange Pound Cake

Fine-textured pound cakes are made by beating soft butter and sugar until fluffy, then beating in the eggs to form an emulsion and finally stirring in the flour.

unsalted butter for greasing pan, plus ¾ cup (6 oz/185 g), at room temperature
1¼ cups (5 oz/155 g) cake (soft-wheat) flour

¾ teaspoon baking powder
tiny pinch of salt
1 orange
¾ cup (6 oz/185 g) sugar
3 eggs, lightly beaten

Preheat an oven to 350°F (180°C). Butter an 8½-by-4½-inch (21.5-by-11.5-cm) loaf pan, and line the bottom and two long sides with parchment paper, allowing the paper to extend over the pan sides slightly; then butter the paper.

In a small bowl, combine the flour, baking powder and salt; set aside. Zest the orange (see page 9); mince the zest finely and set aside. Place the ¾ cup (6 oz/185 g) butter and the sugar in a large bowl. Using an electric mixer, beat until light and fluffy (see top photo), about 5 minutes, stopping occasionally to scrape down the bowl sides. Gradually beat in the eggs (see bottom photo). Stir in the orange zest. Sift the flour mixture over the butter mixture and beat until smooth. Pour the batter into the prepared pan. Using a rubber spatula, smooth the top, then make a lengthwise slit 1 inch (2.5 cm) deep down the middle to minimize splitting as the batter rises during baking.

Bake until golden brown and a toothpick inserted in the center comes out clean, 40–45 minutes. Let cool in the pan on a rack for 10 minutes, then invert onto the rack and peel off the paper. Turn right side up and let cool completely.

Transfer to a serving plate. Cut into slices to serve.

Makes 1 loaf cake; serves 6

MAKING TRUFFLES

FORMING TRUFFLES
Using a pastry bag fitted with a plain tip, pipe 1-inch (2.5-cm) mounds well spaced on a prepared baking sheet.

MELTING CHOCOLATE FOR COATING
Do not melt chocolate too quickly or allow it to come in contact with the water in the saucepan or it will become grainy.

DIPPING THE TRUFFLES
Dip the chilled truffles into the melted chocolate to coat. Place on a lined baking sheet to refrigerate until set.

Chocolate Truffles

FOR THE TRUFFLES:
½ lb (250 g) bittersweet
    chocolate, finely chopped
1 oz (30 g) unsweetened
    chocolate, finely chopped
½ cup (4 fl oz/125 ml) milk
2 tablespoons unsalted butter,
    at room temperature
2 tablespoons dark rum,
    Cognac or Grand Marnier

FOR THE COATING:
6 oz (185 g) bittersweet
    chocolate, finely chopped
½ oz (15 g) unsweetened
    chocolate, finely chopped
1 tablespoon vegetable oil
unsweetened cocoa

To make the truffles, place the chocolates in a bowl. In a saucepan over medium heat, bring the milk to a boil, then remove from the heat and let cool for 5 minutes. Pour over the chocolate and stir until melted and smooth. Stir in the butter and liquor. Refrigerate, stirring occasionally, just until firm enough to hold a shape, 15–20 minutes.

Line a baking sheet with aluminum foil. Fit a pastry bag with a plain ½-inch (12-mm) round tip. Transfer the chocolate mixture to the bag and twist the top securely. Pipe the chocolate onto the prepared baking sheet (see top photo). Flatten the peaks with a fingertip and refrigerate, uncovered, until firm, about 2 hours.

To make the coating, place the chocolates in a metal bowl. Fill a saucepan one-fourth full with water and bring to a simmer over low heat. Set the bowl over (not touching) the water in the pan and melt the chocolates, stirring occasionally (see center photo). Stir in the oil. Remove the pan from the heat.

Using your hands, quickly roll the mounds of chocolate into rounds. Using a fork, dip the rounds into the melted chocolate (see bottom photo), then refrigerate until set, about 20 minutes.

Sift the cocoa over the truffles to dust lightly. Serve immediately, or cover and refrigerate in a single layer for up to 3 days.

Makes about 25 truffles

Glossary

The following glossary defines basic cooking ingredients used throughout this book.

ANCHOVIES
Tiny saltwater fish, related to sardines, most commonly found as canned fillets that have been salted and preserved in oil. Anchovies packed in salt are considered the finest; rinse before using.

BEANS
Among the most common bean varieties are chick-peas, the round, tan members of the pea family (below right), with a slightly crunchy texture and nutlike flavor. Also known as garbanzo or ceci beans. Kidney beans (below) are popular kidney-shaped beans with brownish red skins, slightly mealy texture and robust flavor. White kidney beans are also available. White (navy) beans are small, white, thin-skinned oval beans also known as soldier or Boston beans.

BELL PEPPERS
Sweet-fleshed, bell-shaped member of the pepper family. Also known as capsicum. Most common in the unripe green form, although ripened red or yellow varieties are also available.

BUTTER
For the recipes in this book, unsalted butter is preferred. Lacking salt, it allows the cook greater leeway in seasoning recipes to taste.

CAPERS
Small, pickled buds of a bush common to the Mediterranean, generally used whole as a savory flavoring or garnish.

CHEESES
Some basic types used in this book include:

Blue Cheese
Blue-veined cheeses of many varieties have rich, tangy flavors and creamy to crumbly consistencies. Varieties include Roquefort, Gorgonzola and Maytag blue, an American blue cheese (below).

Cheddar Cheese
Firm, smooth whole-milk cheese, pale yellow-white to deep yellow-orange. Ranges in taste from mild and sweet when young to rich and sharply tangy when aged.

Cream Cheese
Smooth, white, mild-tasting cheese made from cream and milk, used on its own as a spread or as an ingredient that adds rich flavor and texture to recipes.

Gruyère
Variety of Swiss cheese (right) with a firm, smooth texture, small holes and a relatively strong flavor.

Monterey Jack
Mild, slightly tangy semisoft cheese made from whole, partly skimmed or skimmed cow's milk.

Mascarpone
A thick Italian cream cheese usually sold in tubs; similar to French crème fraîche. Look for mascarpone in the cheese case of an Italian delicatessen or specialty-food shop.

Parmesan
Thick-crusted Italian cow's milk cheese with a sharp, salty, full flavor resulting from at least two years of aging. Buy in block form (below), to grate fresh as needed. The finest Italian variety is designated Parmigiano-Reggiano®.

CHILI PEPPERS
A wide variety of fresh chilies may be found in well-stocked food stores and ethnic markets. Some common types include Anaheim chilies (below), also known as New Mexico or long green chilies,

which are mild to moderately hot, slender and about 6 inches (15 cm) long. Jalapeño chilies (below) are small, thick-fleshed, fiery chilies, usually sold green, although red ripened specimens may sometimes be found. Poblano chilies are mild-to-hot and resemble tapered, triangular bell peppers. Poblanos range in color from dark green when young to red when ripe. See page 13 for advice on handling chilies.

CORNSTARCH
Fine, powdery flour ground from the endosperm of corn—the white heart of the kernel—and, because it contains no gluten, used as a thickening agent in some sauces, stir-fries and stews. Also known as cornflour.

CREAM, HEAVY
Whipping cream with a butterfat content of at least 36 percent. In Britain, use double cream.

EGGS
Although eggs are sold in the United States in a range of standard sizes, large eggs are the most common size and should be used for the recipes in this book.

FLOURS
All-purpose flour (also called plain flour) is the most common flour for baking, consisting of a blend of hard and soft wheats. It is sold in its natural, pale yellow unbleached form or bleached, the result of a chemical process that not only whitens it, but also makes it easier to blend with higher percentages of fat and sugar. Bleached flour is therefore commonly used for recipes where more tender results are desired, while unbleached flour yields more crisp results.

Unbleached bread flour is ground from the endosperm of hard wheat, yielding a high-gluten product ideal for bread.

Cake flour is very fine-textured bleached flour for use in cakes and other baked goods. Also called soft-wheat flour. All-purpose flour is not an acceptable substitute.

MUSHROOMS
A wide variety of cultivated and wild mushrooms are available in most food stores. Small, cultivated white and brown mushrooms (right) are the most common.

Shiitake mushrooms, a meaty-flavored Asian variety (below), have flat, dark brown caps usually 2–3 inches (5–7.5 cm) in diameter. Commonly sold dried but available fresh with increasing frequency in Asian food shops. Also available dried.

Portobello mushrooms have wide, flat, deep-brown caps, a rich, mildly meaty taste and a silken texture. Cremini, which are immature portobellos, have the same coloring but a shape more closely resembling cultivated mushrooms.

MUSTARD, DIJON
Dijon mustard is made in Dijon, France, from brown mustard seeds (unless marked *blanc*) and white wine or wine vinegar. Pale in color, fairly hot and sharp tasting, true Dijon mustard and non-French blends labeled Dijon-style are widely available.

NUTS
Rich and mellow in flavor, crisp and crunchy in texture, a wide variety of nuts complements sweet and savory recipes alike.

Almonds are mellow, sweet nuts. An important crop in California and used throughout the world, almonds are sold whole (left) and, for baking purposes, the nuts are commonly sold already skinless (blanched) and cut into slivers or slices (flakes).

Pecans are brown-skinned, crinkly textured nuts with a distinctive sweet, rich flavor and crisp, slightly crumbly texture. They are native to the southern United States.

HERBS
Many fresh and dried herbs alike can be used to bring bright, lively flavor to savory dishes. Those used in this book include:

Basil
Sweet, spicy herb popular in Italian and French cooking.

Bay Leaves
Dried whole leaves of the bay laurel tree (below). Pungent and spicy, they flavor simmered dishes, marinades and pickling mixtures.

Chervil
Herb with small leaves resembling flat-leaf (Italian) **parsley** and with a subtle flavor reminiscent of both parsley and anise.

Chives
Long, thin green shoots with a mild flavor resembling onions, to which they are related.

Cilantro
Green, leafy herb (below) resembling flat-leaf (Italian) **parsley,** with a sharp, aromatic, somewhat astringent flavor. Popular in Latin American and Asian cuisines. Also called fresh coriander and commonly referred to as Chinese parsley.

Dill
Fine, feathery leaves with a sweet, aromatic flavor. Sold fresh (left) or dried.

Herbes de Provence
A commercially sold dried herb blend typical of the Provence region of south-central France; it may include **rosemary, thyme,** savory and such other local seasonings as **oregano, basil** and lavender blossoms.

Marjoram
Pungent, aromatic herb used dried or fresh to season meats, poultry, seafood and vegetables.

Mint
Refreshing herb (below) available in many varieties, with spearmint the most common. Used fresh.

Oregano
Aromatic, pungent and spicy Mediterranean herb (left)—also known as wild **marjoram**—used fresh or dried as a savory seasoning.

Parsley
This popular fresh herb is available in two varieties, the readily available curly-leaf type and a flat-leaf type. The latter, also known as Italian parsley, has a more pronounced flavor and is preferred.

Rosemary
Mediterranean herb (below), used either fresh or dried, with an aromatic flavor especially well suited to meats and poultry. Strong in flavor, it should be used sparingly, except when grilling.

Sage
Pungent herb, used either fresh or dried, that goes particularly well with meats and poultry.

Tarragon
Fragrant, distinctively sweet herb (below) used fresh or dried as a seasoning for salads, seafood, chicken, meats, eggs and vegetables.

Thyme
Fragrant, clean-tasting, small-leaved herb popular fresh or dried as a seasoning for poultry, light meats, seafood and vegetables.

Pine nuts (below) are small, ivory seeds extracted from the cones of a species of pine tree, with a rich, slightly resinous flavor.

OILS

Oils are used for cooking and/or to subtly enhance the flavor of recipes in which they are used. Store all oils in airtight containers away from heat and light.

Extra-virgin olive oil, extracted from olives on the first pressing without use of heat or chemicals, is prized for its pure, fruity taste and golden to pale green hue. The higher-priced extra-virgin olive oils usually are of better quality.

Products labeled pure olive oil, less aromatic and flavorful, may be used for all-purpose cooking.

Flavorless vegetable and seed oils such as safflower and corn oil are employed for their high cooking temperatures and bland flavor.

OLIVES

Throughout Mediterranean Europe, ripe black olives are cured in combinations of salt and seasonings alone; in brines; in vinegars; or in oils to produce a wide range of pungently flavored results. Good-quality cured olives, such as French Niçoise, Greek Kalamata (below) or Italian Gaeta, are available in ethnic delicatessens, specialty-food shops and well-stocked food stores.

ONIONS

All manner of onions are used to enhance the flavor of savory recipes.

Green onions, also called spring onions or scallions, are a variety harvested immature, leaves and all, before their bulbs have formed. The green and white parts may both be enjoyed, raw or cooked, for their mild but still pronounced onion flavor.

Yellow onions are the common, white-fleshed, strong-flavored variety distinguished by their dry, yellowish brown skins.

Pearl onions are small but pungent onions, about ¾ inch (2 cm) in diameter; also known as pickling onions, that are prepared as a side dish on their own or added whole to stews and braises.

PANCETTA

Unsmoked bacon cured with salt and pepper. May be sold flat or rolled into a large sausage shape. Unroll and slice or chop before using.

PASTAS

Of the more than 400 distinct commercial Italian-style pasta shapes, two of the most common ones, used in this book, are ribbon-shaped fettuccine and the classic rods known as spaghetti. Egg noodles, also found in the dried-pasta section of food stores, are short, narrow to medium ribbons made from flour-and-egg dough.

POLENTA

Italian term for specially ground coarse cornmeal and for the mush that results from its cooking. The latter may be enriched with butter, cream, cheese or eggs. When cold,

POTATOES

Potatoes contain a significant amount of starch that can be removed by soaking the raw potato in water to improve the texture in some recipes. While the kinds of potatoes and the names they go by vary from region to region, some common varieties include:

Baking potatoes

Large potatoes with thick brown skins that have a dry, mealy texture when cooked. Also known as russet or Idaho potatoes.

White boiling potatoes

Medium-sized potatoes with thin tan skins, such as the White Rose variety. When cooked, their textures are finer than baking potatoes but coarser than yellow-tinged waxy varieties.

Red potatoes

White-fleshed potatoes with thin red skins and waxy flesh. Can be used for steaming, roasting or boiling.

Yellow potatoes

Any of a variety of thin-skinned potatoes with yellow-tinged, waxy flesh well suited to steaming, boiling, roasting or sautéing. The Yukon Gold variety is widely regarded as one of the finest, for its bright yellow flesh and rich, almost buttery flavor.

Red potato

Baking potato

White boiling potato

it has a consistency firm enough for it to be shaped and grilled or fried.

PROSCIUTTO

This raw ham is a specialty of Parma, Italy. It is cured by dry-salting for one month, followed by air-drying in cool curing sheds for half a year or longer.

SHELLFISH

Many varieties of shellfish and crustaceans are sold in well-stocked seafood markets. When purchased, shellfish should have only the fresh, clean scent of the sea, and should show no signs of poor handling.

Mussels are bluish black–shelled bivalves prized for their sweet, orange-pink flesh. They should only be purchased live. (See page 45 for directions on handling.)

The bivalve mollusks known as scallops come in two common varieties: the round flesh of sea scallops is usually 1½ inches (4 cm) in diameter, while the bay scallop (below) is considerably smaller. Both are usually sold already shelled.

Raw shrimp (prawns) are generally sold with the heads already removed but the shells still intact. Peel and devein before using (see page 46 for directions).

SOY SAUCE

Asian seasoning and condiment made from soybeans, wheat, salt and water. Seek out good-quality imported soy sauces; Chinese brands tend to be saltier than Japanese. Those labeled "dark" soy sauce have a fuller, richer flavor.

SPICES

Savory or sweet seasonings derived from the dried seeds, roots, barks or stamens of plants, spices enliven a broad range of dishes.

Cumin is a Middle Eastern spice with a strong, dusky, aromatic flavor. It is sold ground or as whole, small, crescent-shaped seeds.

Nutmeg (below), a popular baking spice, is the hard pit of the fruit of the nutmeg tree. It may be bought already ground or, for fresher flavor, whole to be grated as needed.

Golden-orange saffron (below) is an intensely aromatic spice made from the dried stigmas of a species of crocus. It offers a delicate perfume and golden hue to foods and is sold either as threads—the dried stigmas—or in powdered form. Look for products labeled pure saffron.

The most common of all spices, pepper is best purchased as whole peppercorns (below), to be ground in a pepper mill as needed, or coarsely crushed. Pungent black peppercorns derive from slightly underripe pepper berries, whose hulls oxidize as they dry. Milder white peppercorns come from fully ripened berries, with the husks removed before drying.

SUGARS

Many different forms of sugar may be used to sweeten recipes.

Brown sugar is a rich-tasting granulated sugar combined with molasses in varying quantities to yield golden, light or dark brown sugar. With crystals varying from coarse to finely granulated, brown sugar is widely available in the baking section of food stores.

Confectioners' sugar is finely pulverized sugar, also known as powdered or icing sugar. It dissolves quickly when combined with liquid to provide a thin, white decorative coating. To prevent confectioners' sugar from absorbing moisture in the air and caking, manufacturers often mix a little **cornstarch** into it.

The standard, widely used form of pure white sugar is known as granulated sugar. When ground to form extra-fine granules that dissolve quickly in liquids, it is known as superfine sugar; in Britain, use castor sugar.

TOMATOES

During summer, when tomatoes are in season, use the best red or yellow sun-ripened tomatoes you can find. At other times of year, plum tomatoes, sometimes called Roma or egg tomatoes, are likely to have the best flavor and texture; for cooking, canned whole plum tomatoes are also good.

Sun-dried tomatoes (below), available either dry or packed in oil with or without herbs and

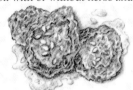

spices, have an intense, sweet-tart flavor and a pleasantly chewy texture that enhance some savory recipes.

Tomato paste is a commercial concentrate of puréed tomatoes, often sold in small cans, used to add flavor and body to sauces.

VANILLA EXTRACT

Vanilla beans, the long and slender dried aromatic pods of a variety of orchid, are one of the most popular flavorings in dessert making. Vanilla is most commonly used in the form of an alcohol-based extract (essence); be sure to purchase products labeled pure vanilla extract.

VINEGARS

Literally "sour wine," vinegar results when certain strains of yeast cause wine—or some other alcoholic liquid—to ferment for a second time, turning it acidic. The best-quality wine vinegars begin with good-quality wine.

Red wine vinegar, like the wine from which it is made, has a more robust flavor than vinegar produced from white wine.

Balsamic vinegar, a specialty of Modena, Italy, is made from reduced grape juice and aged for many years.

YEAST

One of the most widely available forms of yeast for baking, active-dry yeast is commonly sold in individual packages containing 2¼ teaspoons (¼ oz/7 g) and found in the baking section of food stores. To save time, quick-rise yeast, which can raise breads and cakes in as little as half the normal time, is preferred in some recipes. If using fresh cake yeast, substitute ½ oz (15 g) for 1 envelope active dry yeast. (See page 87 for essential yeast dough techniques.)

WINES AND SPIRITS

Whether used in marinades or as part of the cooking liquid, all manner of wines and spirits lend their distinctive flavors and aromas to recipes. Those used in this book are:

Cognac

Dry spirit distilled from wine and, strictly speaking, produced in the Cognac region of France. Good-quality dry wine-based brandies may be substituted.

Grand Marnier

A popular commercial brand of orange-flavored liqueur, distinguished by its pure Cognac base.

Marsala

Dry or sweet amber Italian wine from the area of Marsala, on the island of Sicily.

Rum, Dark

Dark amber spirit that carries some of the caramel color and distinctive flavor of the sugarcane or molasses from which it is distilled. Light rum varieties are also available.

Sherry, Dry

Fortified, cask-aged wine, enjoyed on its own as an aperitif and used as a flavoring in both savory and sweet recipes.

Wines

All manner of table wines, from dry whites and reds to sweet dessert wines and Champagne, may be included in recipes. Note that it is always best to cook with a wine that you would also consider good enough to drink; its finer character will be imparted to the finished dish.

Index

ACKNOWLEDGMENTS
The publishers would like to thank the following people for their generous assistance and support in producing this book:
Ken DellaPenta, Tina Schmitz, Marguerite Ozburn and the managers of Williams-Sonoma stores.
The following kindly lent props for the photography: Biordi Art Imports and Fillamento.

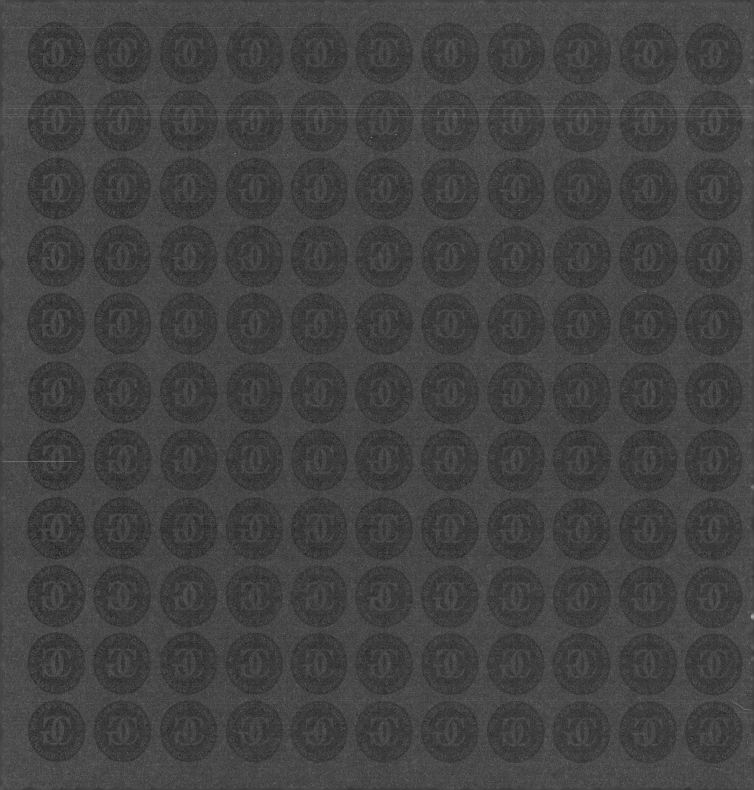